The
RESEARCH SYSTEM
IN THE 1980'S

PUBLIC POLICY ISSUES

John M. Logsdon, ed.

THE FRANKLIN INSTITUTE PRESS

© 1982 by THE FRANKLIN INSTITUTE

Published by THE FRANKLIN INSTITUTE PRESS^{SM}
Philadelphia, Pennsylvania

Current printing (last digit):
5   4   3   2   1

Printed in the United States of America

Library of Congress Cataloging in Publication Data

The Research system in the 1980's.

   Includes bibliographical references.
   Contents: Introduction / John M. Logsdon -- Basic research on campus / Steven Muller -- Science, government, and policy / Emmanuel R. Piore -- [etc.]
   1. Research--United States--Addresses, essays, lectures. I. Logsdon, John M., 1937-
Q180.U5R398   001.4'0973   82-5029
ISBN 0-89168-044-6   AACR2

Acknowledgements

Most of the papers in this volume were first presented at one of the meetings of a science policy seminar organized by the Graduate Program in Science, Technology, and Public Policy of the George Washington University between January 1980 and January 1981. These seminar meetings provided an opportunity for Washington-based professionals involved in science and technology policy to meet on a regular basis; the average seminar attendance was 65 professionals and 12 graduate students. Funds for these seminars and for partial support of the publication of these seminar proceedings were provided by National Science Foundation grant PRA-7922821 from the Division of Policy Research and Analysis. Thanks are due to NSF seminar program managers Robert Trumble and Elmina Johnson and to PRA Director Alden Bean.

Planning for the seminar series was guided by a distinguished advisory committee which included:

John Holmfeld, Science Policy Consultant,
Committee on Science and Technology,
U.S. House of Representatives
Honorable Charles A. Mosher,
Former Member of Congress
Gail Pesyna, then with the staff of the
President's Commission on a National Agenda for the 80s
Thomas Ratchford, Associate Executive Officer,
American Association for the Advancement of Science
Albert H. Teich, Science Policy Studies Manager,
American Association for the Advancement of Science

Paper topics and speakers for the seminar were selected with the advice of this group. Two of the papers, those by Nelkin and Heising-Goodman, were commissioned after a national competition for which members of the advisory committee acted as reviewers. Thus I owe several different debts of thanks to these individuals.

Kimberly K. Lutz was in charge of organizing the seminar meetings and of preparing these proceedings for publication; simply put, she was invaluable. Most of the final typing was done by Jody Curtis. Both made my editorial tasks much easier. I would also like to acknowledge the fine work of Marcia Wertime, who edited the papers for The Franklin Institute Press. Of course, any opinions, findings, conclusions, or recommendations expressed in the papers in this volume are those of the authors, and do not necessarily reflect the views of NSF or the editor.

The comments of those attending the science policy seminar series suggest that it has provided a useful forum for the exchange of views on topics of high concern to the Washington policy community. I hope this volume is equally useful to those outside Washington interested in the vitality of the U.S. research system.

John M. Logsdon

Contents

Contents

Introduction: the Research System Under Stress

John M. Logsdon

In its perceptive analysis of the initial research and development (R&D) policy and budget decisions of the Reagan administration, the American Association for the Advancement of Science notes that the United States has reached a "fundamental turning point"[1] in the relationship between the federal government and the nation's scientific and technological enterprise. The essays in this volume provide detailed confirmation of this observation.

However, it is important to distinguish between two types of change in the government-science connection. One is a shorter-term reflection of the country's current economic problems and the commitment of a new, conservative government to drastic reductions in federal spending and in federal involvement with society in general. Science will not be exempt from this commitment and there are bound to be significant shifts in the patterns of federal support for research and development during the time Ronald Reagan is in the White House. But these changes are likely to be less far-reaching in their impacts than the results of the trends and pressures discussed in this volume will be.

The synergistic interaction of government and the U.S. research system was largely a product of experiences during World War II and the immediate post-War years, and it was modified by the pressures of the Cold War and the U.S. reaction to Sputnik in the fifties. The patterns of that relationship were such that in 1961 Don K. Price could write that science was "the only institution for which tax funds are appropriated almost on faith and under concordats which protect the autonomy of the laboratory."[2]

No more. As one after another of the papers in this collection point out, major changes in today's government-science relationship include: *1.* the breakdown in faith that the products of the research system are *prima facie* good for society and thus deserving of continually increasing public support, and *2.* attempts to modify the "autonomy of the laboratory" (and of the universities in which many laboratories are located) in ways which give to public officials more control over the pur-

John M. Logsdon is the Director of the Graduate Program in Science, Technology, and Public Policy at George Washington University, where he is also a Professor of Political Science and Public Affairs.

poses for which tax funds supporting science are allocated and over the ways in which those allocations are spent.

The focus of the papers in this collection is on the *research system,* defined as the set of institutions, facilities, and most importantly, people, whose activities both increase society's storehouse of knowledge about physical, biological, and social reality and investigate ways in which that knowledge can be used for human purposes. In the definition used here, the mechanisms through which such activities are supported by both government and the private sector are also part of the research system. Little direct attention is given to issues involving the utilization of research results, such as industrial innovation, technology assessment, or identification of environmental risks, although clearly the health of the research enterprise is a crucial component of these broader concerns.

Summary of Individual Papers

Perhaps the best way to communicate the range of issues addressed in this volume is by discussing briefly the major themes and perspectives of each of the papers it contains. Based on this discussion, it should be possible to identify the principal sources of stress on the research system, stress which may threaten the performance of what has become in the last 35 years the world's most productive source of new scientific discoveries.

Dorothy Nelkin's paper, "Public Attitudes and the Control of Research", sets the stage for the volume by pointing out how intimately the practice of science, as a major human activity, is linked to the context of social values and power relationships in which it takes place. Nelkin is a long-time student of the interactions of technology and society; in this paper she turns her attention to rising demands from society for control, not only of applications of technology, but also of scientific research. These demands stem primarily from a concern over the social and ethical implications of the *uses* of science, but also from the value dimensions of some areas of science itself, particularly in biological and social science. Nelkin raises a spectre which haunts many contemporary scientists — that the call for influence over the selection of research topics and research methods can lead quickly to establishing "limits of inquiry," i.e., areas of forbidden knowledge.[3] While she dismisses this concern as not well grounded, at least for the time being, Nelkin argues that finding ways for incorporating social values into the decision process, with respect to scientific priorities and support levels when public funds are involved, is not only unavoidable but socially desirable. She believes that issues of participation, equity, and ethics should be considered along with issues of scientific merit in research policy decisions. Nelkin seems less concerned than most of the other authors about a possible shift away from the relative autonomy of the scientific community, arguing that "the complex and esoteric nature of many decisions concerning science, the very real difficulty in coming to grip with ethical issues, and the continued faith in science as a solution to social problems have left control of the research system firmly within the scientific community," since "scientists have been able to control the regulatory process much as industry learned to manage regulation — for its own ends."*

One of the major recipients of federal support for science is Johns Hopkins University in Baltimore, Maryland. The university's president, Steven Muller, in his paper "Basic Research on Campus: A University View," identifies a second major source of stress on the research system, in addition to demands for social control. "Basically," Muller argues, "the problem is money .... Basic research has become such a large-scale and expensive activity as to constitute a heavy drain on federal budgets, and an intolerable financial burden on the American university ... The option of doing basic research on the cheap no longer exists." For at least the past decade, responding in part to the pressures for equity and participation identified by Nelkin and in part to more specific political concerns, federal support of science has been aimed within the limits of scientific merit at the broadest possible geographical distribution of funds. In addition, federal policy has been to support research itself, not the institutions, particularly universities, in which research is carried out. Muller argues that a continuation of the current pattern of research support on a project-by-project basis will lead to a situation in which the major research universities can no longer afford to undertake federally-funded research; he calls for a "fundamental readjustment of the traditional partnership" in which the federal government gives "explicit recognition to the obvious fact that a relatively small group of major research universities already constitute the resource base for most basic research." Muller believes that the government should designate such universities as "national research institutions" in one or more scientific areas and make a "durable federal commitment to assume the full burden of research ... support" in those areas at such institutions.

The project grant system, with awards made on the basis of some form of peer review, has become the major mechanism for government support of academic science; almost half (48 percent in FY 1979) of federal support for research in universities is channeled through a project grant or contract.[4] The project grant was only one of the mechanisms for federal support of basic research developed in the post World War II years, and its rise to dominance reflects the reluctance of the government over the past decade or so to engage in institutional support. Emmanuel Piore, former Chief Scientist and Vice President of IBM, was intimately involved in the development of government-science relationships in the 1945-1960 period, both as a government scientist with the Office of Naval Research,** where he was for a time Chief Scientist, and as a member of the President's Science Advisory Committee in the late 1950's. Piore's paper, "Science, Government, and Policy: A Four-Decade Perspective," is almost nostalgic in tone; he reminds us

---

*Unless otherwise referenced, all quotations are from the papers in this volume.
**Many of the patterns of federal support for science first evolved at the Office of Naval Research.

that "life was simple once," but that "during the past 35 years, as funds have increased and as the number of researchers has increased, life has become more complex. At times the purpose of the original thrust and national policy has become unfocused or even forgotten." That purpose was to provide a climate which would best support the creative activity of individual scientists, and it was with that goal in mind that the various mechanisms for research support, which included funds for constructing large facilities, block grants for the support of a large laboratory and its research staff, support for the acquisition of specialized equipment, and institutional funding for unique organizations, as well as project support for individual investigators, were designed.

What Piore sees and doesn't welcome is the breakdown of the mutual trust, based on personal familiarity as well as on broader forms of interaction, which underlay the original government-science partnership and which is being (has been?) replaced by a much more bureaucratized relationship, with university research administrators dealing with government accountants more frequently than faculty scientists deal with agency program and policy officials. Piore's prescription (which is not likely to be followed in the current policy climate for research) recognizes "a need for greater freedom for scientists to do their work, for less monitoring by the government ... for less monitoring by the non-academic staffs of universities, and for greater involvement of the presidents of our universities." Although a generation separates Emmanuel Piore from Steven Muller, their perceptions of problems and needs in the government-science relationship appear very similar.

A particular source of tension in that relationship, one noted by each of the three preceding authors, are recent demands for increased "accountability" on the part of universities for the ways in which federal research dollars are spent. To many people in universities, government's attempts to change the terms of and requirements for federal research support is a major factor in changing the government-science relationship from a productive partnership to a debilitating confrontation. Although Muller feels that new accountability requirements are only "the tip of the iceberg," more time has been spent over the past few years on this issue than on any other related to federal research policy.

At the heart of the debate concerning accountability is the tradeoff between the existence of adequate controls and reporting requirements sufficient to allow the government to determine whether public funds are being spent wisely, ethically, and fairly, and the existence of a creative and unfettered context for the conduct of scientific inquiry. Both the Executive branch and the Congress appear to have lost some of their earlier faith that universities will act properly as stewards for public funds intended for research support; government's response "is the desire to increase controls over federally-supported work, to enforce existing rules more conscientiously, and to introduce additional rules in areas where difficulties have been encountered," even though many in the research system argue that such a response is as likely to exacerbate the problem as it is to solve it.

One forum in which the issue of accountability received extensive discussion and analysis was the National Commission on Research, an independent (but university-oriented) blue-ribbon group which recently examined various facets of research system operation. Within the Commission, Linda S. Wilson, Associate Vice Chancellor for Research at the University of Illinois, took the lead in evaluating appropriate accountability principles for the 1980's. Her paper, "Accountability in Federally-Supported University Research," both discusses the Commission's findings and recommendation and contains her own analysis of the issue.

Wilson sees the basis of the accountability problem in the "deeply rooted institutional differences between government and research universities," differences which lead to "a serious mismatch of expectations." She decries the deterioration of research relationships between government and universities which has resulted from this mismatch, noting that "the national interest is not served by diminished confidence either in universities, research or the government .... The relationship between the government and the universities involves an interdependence developed over the years as the two have cooperated in pursuit of knowledge for the public welfare. This relationship has been extraordinarily fruitful in scientific achievement."

Wilson's paper includes an analysis of the major policy issues involved in redefining in a positive manner the government-university research relationship; she notes that there can be no perfect solution, given the differences in goals, organizational characteristics, and modes of operation of the two partners. In particular, there is a need to balance the objectives of scientific accountability, which focus on the achievement of results and usually is based on review by scientific peers, and the objectives of financial and administrative reporting, which focus on financial propriety and compliance with administrative regulations. This latter form of accountability seems preferred by government, in part because it can be managed by non-scientific personnel, but universities have strongly resisted government attempts to introduce new accountability requirements which stem from a financial and administrative perspective. Wilson's paper lists the recommendations of the National Commission on Research with respect to accountability; these suggestions stem from the conviction, which is at the heart of her analysis, that "the nation cannot affort to damage universities as institutions by inappropriate and intrusive requirements."

Muller, Piore, and Wilson, seem to share common premises related to the importance of the health of the academic research system; those premises stem from the assumption that it is in society's interests to ensure the conditions under which creative and fundamental science will flourish. Richard Lyon in his paper on "A Bridge Reconnecting Universities and Industry Through Basic Research" reaches a similar conclusion from a different starting point. As Vice President for Petroleum Research at the major laboratory of the nation's largest energy company, Lyon is a "consumer" of research results. He believes that "industry has not benefitted from university basic research to the degree necessary for effective innovation." His paper suggests ways to remedy this situation by developing working and interactive connections — "bridges" — between university researchers and industrial scientists and engineers. Such connections, argues Lyon, can best be created through direct industrial financing of basic research by universities, coupled with close interaction among research performers in the two institutions. The best role for government in this respect, suggests Lyon, is as indirect facilitator rather than as a direct participant in the partnership; in particular, Lyon builds a case for creating significant federal tax incentives aimed at stimulating industrial funding of university basic research. Lyon notes that industry currently supports only about two per cent of university basic research, with most of the rest coming from the federal government. He sets as target a 10-15 percent industry share of the academic research budget as one which would underpin a number of effective industry-university connections.

The match, at the institutional level, between specific industries and specific universities will not be an easy one to make. Lyon lays out some ground rules for an effective connection, but he recognizes that there are bound to be conflicts as well as cooperation in the relationship. He chooses the basic end of the research spectrum as the place to build the connection, since that is where universities have a comparative advantage with respect to other research performers and because "further down the chain of innovation, industry's 'proprietary obsession' conflicts with the academic need to publish."

The importance of an adequate amount of basic research activity to the national well-being is accepted by each of the preceding authors. Moreover, each accepts that the primary supporter of basic science in the United States can only be the government, since, as Lyon suggests, "basic research has a small present value when viewed in cold economic terms, and it is now generally accepted that benefits cannot always be captured by private firms. ... This puts basic research at the economic margin for industry." The notion that support of basic research is an appropriate *public* expenditure has recently come under attack, particularly by conservative economist Milton Friedman. Accepting at face value the claim that most fundamental science does not result in applications with tangible economic or social payoffs for 20 or more years, Friedman asks "what ethical justification do you have for extracting tax money from people for purposes that do not yield them some greater benefit? You have to be able to say that the extra dollar spent on research will produce more than a dollar's worth of benefit to the person from whom the dollar was taken. That is a hard proposition to establish in the case of science."[5]

Mark Pastin, a professional ethicist, provides a provocative and sophisticated response to Friedman's question in his paper "The Scarcity of Ethical Resources: Strategic Planning for Science." Central to Pastin's argument is a rejection of Friedman's assumption that tax dollars must return benefits to those who pay them, rather than to some future beneficiaries. If one allows for a distribution of benefits over time, the question then, according to Pastin, is whether it is *ethical* to prefer present benefits more than future ones, i.e., to use a social discount rate to reduce the value of future benefits when they are compared with current payoffs. He argues that the use of such a discount rate is not ethical, and may in fact be a way of avoiding current sacrifices which only have future payoffs. However, Pastin also argues that there is no ethically ideal way to make strategic decisions (i.e. decisions with consequences mainly in the future) which properly assesses future benefits and costs; thus, he says, society should attempt to make long-term decisions "which approximate ethical ideality within practical constraints."

It is here that basic research spending enters Pastin's argument. He suggests that the most ethically satisfactory actions which are possible now are those which *empower* our successors by "increasing the ability of future generations to produce a life of quality from whatever circumstances we leave for them." Investments in research have had just such an empowering effect, perhaps more so than any alternative investment, and thus Pastin concludes that "there is a definite *ethical* imperative to increase the commitment to R&D." His conclusion, which combines ethics and practicality, is that "the *best* society *will* do is to make future generations better off, in the sense of being more able to meet the challenges of their circumstances."

Given both the practical and the ethical importance of a continuing flow of new knowledge and new ideas from the research system, the observations in Charles Kidd's paper on "New Academic Positions: the Outlook in Europe and North America," are disturbing. Kidd, a veteran observer and analyst of the U.S. research system, notes that "universities in the United States will offer few new academic positions during the 1980's. This creates the prospect that the vigor of basic science will decline unless there is a sustained flow of young people into academic science."

The reasons for this situation are complex; they include the burst of faculty hiring in U.S. universities during the 1960's which has created a large block of tenure-holding professors in their forties who will fill most of the academic slots available for the next decade and more; the prospect of declining undergraduate enrollments which implies the need for few new academic positions; and the slowdown in research funding for universities, which also puts a limit on the growth rate of faculty and graduate student research activity. Kidd notes that similar difficulties exist in Canada and in most European countries, and his paper examines the responses of those countries to the problem of maintaining the vigor of their fundamental research efforts. While Kidd finds that the approaches of some European countries may indeed be relevant to the U.S. situation, he cautions that the shortage of academic positions is "not an isolated phenomenon but ... part of a complex of science policy issues." Thus, says Kidd, what is needed are "general measures designed to sustain the vitality of national basic research systems," not piecemeal responses to specific problems.

Of course, basic research is only part of the total U.S. research system; from the point of view of overall benefits to society, the other elements of the system, particularly the engineering enterprise, are at least equally significant. The vitality of the country's engineering capabilities, except as they relate directly to government objectives such as national defense and space exploration, has been the focus of less attention in terms of public policy than has the health of academic science. In large part, this is because almost 80 percent of U.S.

engineers are employed by industry, and thus the status of the engineering profession, engineering education, and engineering research have tended to be viewed as concerns primarily of the private sector.

This emphasis is misplaced, says F. Karl Willenbrock in his paper, "Engineering, The Neglected Ingredient." Willenbrock was formerly the director of a major government engineering laboratory at the National Bureau of Standards and is now dean of a large engineering school, and thus his analysis proceeds from an informed and broadly gauged perspective. The core of that analysis is that "while in many technologies the United States is at the forefront of new developments, there are definite indications that U.S. engineering is not in a healthy state." He also asserts that "engineering is so basic to the development of society's essential technologies that the country cannot allow it to be weakened by chronic unsolved problems, or by public policies inimical to further development."

Willenbrock's paper is a detailed and comprehensive analysis of the current state of engineering in the United States. He identifies three problem areas in which more effective public policies could improve the situation: the first is *engineering education,* about which he echoes Steven Muller's complaint about basic research support, saying that "although much of the higher education system in the U.S. suffers from underfunding, this problem is particularly acute in engineering." He calls for a tripartite government-industry-university attack on this problem; the second is the *inadequate availability of engineering manpower,* where again a tripartite approach seems optimal to ensure the buildup of the engineering capacity required in the national interest; the third area is those *static technological fields* in which neither government nor industry is investing adequate R&D resources but which are important to the country. Willenbrock argues that "while it is not reasonable to assume that U.S. technology will lead the world in all fields, it is important that the United States be near the leading position in technical areas of fundamental importance to the U.S. industrial economy and its national defense." He identifies optics, steel, automobiles, and consumer electronics as such areas.

The final paper in this volume is different in focus than its predecessors. Prepared by Carolyn Heising-Goodman, a specialist in energy economics and risk analysis, the paper argues for the value of "Quantitative Methods in R&D Decision-Making." Heising-Goodman's paper suggests how a Bayesian decision analysis approach to assessing the consequences of new technological applications can meet "the challenge of integrating quantitative data, scientific methods and expertise into the political process, where many of the country's major R&D decisions are made." While she recognizes the influence of non-scientific factors on that process, she also argues that "decisions should at least be based in part on the best technical studies available. The alternative is to always defer to majority rule, no matter how misguided." Analysts, she believes, "can only continue to perform the studies and hope that somebody listens."

Some General Themes

Earlier in this paper, I cited Don K. Price's 1961 description of the autonomy of the scientific community, as it prospered with government support; it is instructive to quote another of Price's observations, made almost two decades later: "some scientists are almost tempted to regret the implicit bargain on which massive federal research has been based since the Second World War."[6] Certainly there is evidence of such regret in several of the papers in this book. While recognizing the dependence of the scientific enterprise upon federal funding, the leaders of the scientific community are becoming increasingly uncomfortable as what was once implicit — the terms of the government-science bargain — become explicit. In the period between 1945-1960, it was possible to create a partnership between the government-scientific communities based on mutually-agreed-upon, but not specified, understandings both because the funding levels were not enormous and because the World War II experience had created bonds of mutual confidence and personal familiarity between leaders in both communities. There was little questioning of the methods for allocation of public money for science, with scientists themselves exercising primary control over the disbursement and spending of that money.

In a sense, science and technology are victims of their own successes. As their power to shape contemporary life has become evident and as society's investments in R&D have become very large (in absolute terms if not in percentage of national wealth), it is no longer possible to manage the relationship between government and science over lunch at the Cosmos Club. The public and its representatives, conscious of the money and the potential effects of these investments, will continue to demand more control. Much of the turmoil in the research system which is reflected in this volume is a result of attempts by leaders in government and in research to adjust to those demands by the public, while at the same time maintaining what they believe to be essential conditions for scientific productivity.

In particular, current public scrutiny of the relationship between government and academic science is both revealing the substantial differences in goals and expectations between the two partners and highlighting the difficulty in finding patterns of interactions which can be articulated explicitly and which are acceptable to both actors. There is a dilemma here, but it is not an insoluble one. For example, while Muller and Willenbrock argue for both increased federal funding levels and new patterns of research support and Nelkin's conclusion is that the demands for increased public control will not disappear, it does appear as if there is enough recognition of common interests to support the difficult process of renegotiating the government-science "bargain" on terms appropriate for the 1980's. The work of the National Commission on Research discussed in Wilson's paper is one element in this renegotiation process, but the work required has really only just begun and will be a major item on the science policy agenda for the 1980's.

The dominant influences on national science policy for the past four decades has come from leadership of the academic science community, with the White House science office, the National Science Foundation, the National Institutes of Health, and the National Academy of Sciences serving as bridges between academic and political leaders. Now a new influence is emerging in the form of industrial leaders. A tentative courtship between universities and industry, with the federal government serving as matchmaker, has been underway for the past seveal years. As different in goals and expectations as government and universities are, perhaps universities and industry are even more dissimilar; this means that involving industry as a major partner in the U.S. research system, beyond the industrial suport of its own R&D activities, is going to be very difficult, particularly when this match must be consummated in the light of public scrutiny.

The links between industry and engineering schools are more firmly established than those between business and academic science, but, as Willenbrock's paper suggests, even those links are not functioning very well and are likely to require the involvement of a third partner, government, for repair. The attempts to forge a three-way partnership between government, industry, and universities in order to make the U.S. research system more productive present a major challenge to institutional creativity; responses to this challenge will be another significant item of the 1980's science policy agenda.

A more muted theme than those just discussed, but nevertheless an important one in several of the papers in this volume, is the need for U.S. research policy to be formulated in an international context. There are two major reasons for this requirement: first, creative research and the productive utilization of its results will continue to increase in importance to the U.S. economy, to the quality of living in this country, and to national security; and second, other countries, through government policies among other means, are stimulating their research systems and outperforming the United States in crucial areas of science and technology.

The superb performance of its research system has significantly helped the United States to exercise a position of world leadership in the post World War II period. Effective public policies have been a major reason for this performance, and the papers in this collection suggest that even more effective public policy initiatives are needed to sustain such a performance. To the extent that the stresses identified in this volume threaten the country's ability to maintain a superior level of accomplishment, they also threaten the achievement of a number of nonscientific values central to the national interest. This is perhaps the fundamental reason why the vitality of the U.S. research system should be a leading item of the public policy agenda for the 1980's.

REFERENCES

1. Willis H. Shapley, Albert H. Teich, and Gail J. Breslow, *Research and Development: AAAS Report VI* (Washington: American Association for the Advancement of Science, 1981), p. 17.

2. Don K. Price, "The Scientific Establishment," *Science,* August 18, 1961, p. 1099.

3 .See the Spring 1978 issue of *Daedalus* for a discussion of the potential limits of scientific inquiry.

4. Willis Shapley, *et al, Research and Development: AAAS Report V* (Washington: American Association for the Advancement of Science, 1980), p. 89.

5. Friedman is quoted in *Science,* October 3, 1980, p. 33.

6. Don K. Price, "Endless Frontier or Bureaucratic Morass?" *Daedalus,* Vol. 107, No. 2 (1978), p. 75.

Public Attitudes and the Control of Research

Dorothy Nelkin

The scientific inquiries of Frederick II of Hohenstausen, King of Sicily and Holy Roman Emperor in the early thirteenth century, are famous. He wrote an authoritative manual on hunting with falcons, which was filled with detailed zoological observations. He also performed a number of experiments to discover the natural origin of language. In one case, he placed children in the care of nurses who were under strict orders not to talk to their charges in order to discover whether they would learn to speak Hebrew, Greek, Latin, or Arabic. The children died. In another experiment, he cut open human subjects to find out whether people digest better if they rest or exercise after eating. Obviously Frederick used public funds for his research, and was accountable neither to Institutional Review Boards, nor to guidelines for human experimentation. Social values and the existing power relationship in that society simply allowed for such research practices.

This dependence of science upon contemporary social values and existing power relationships is important to consider, as this paper explores the effect of recent public attitudes on research policy and, in particular, on the control of scientific research. This consideration will govern the analysis as this paper first reviews the nature of recent challenges to the research system and then explores their impact on the funding and the control of research.

Challenges to the Research System

Looking back at the key events in science policy over the past decade, one is struck by the remarkable number of protests which expressed growing public concern about the social and ethical implications of science and technology. While many of the controversies of the 1970's focused on technology and the application of science, the research process itself has also been under recent, critical scrutiny. Indeed, many of the assumptions that shaped the research system after World War II have been seriously questioned.

Dorothy Nelkin is a professor at Cornell University, where she holds a joint appointment in the Science, Technology, and Society program, the Department of City and Regional Planning, and the Department of Sociology.

This particular research system was devised by the scientists themselves, and it allowed for an amazing degree of self-governance. Since there was no well-worked out and comprehensive science policy to establish priorities and political relationships, the direction of science was guided by science advisory groups at every level of government. And like any other representative bodies, these acted with an eye to the interests of their clientele. Thus, Don Price called science "the only institution for which tax funds are appropriated almost on faith and under concordats which protect the autonomy of the laboratory."[1] This delegation of authority was based on several beliefs: first, that fundamental research has intrinsic value and should be supported simply on grounds of scientific merit; second, that the results of such research are useful in the long run for the implementation of societal goals; third, that the scientific community, guided by norms of neutral, apolitical behavior, is able to regulate itself in a disinterested manner; and, finally, that externally-imposed constraints would only impede science at considerable cost to society.

Any delegation of authority over decisions which concern publicly funded activities is necessarily fragile, and indeed there appears to be a trend towards an increasingly closer control over science. In an extended study of research relationships, the National Commission on Research identified "accountability" as the key problematic issue in the present system.[2] At a recent Nobel Symposium, Donald Frederickson, then the Director of the National Institutes of Health, outlined several trends towards greater accountability. These include: increased Congressional interest in health-related research; government-wide legislation over issues, such as freedom of information, that effect the management of research; a growing body of legislative and administrative law in such diverse areas as human experimentation and toxic substances control that change the context of research; and rising public demands to assess science on the basis of economic, ethical, and social factors.[3]

Such pressures for accountability and, indeed, for a social assessment of science reflect important changes in public attitudes towards science. Surveys suggest continued public support for science, but they suggest a certain ambivalence as well. Optimistic expectations are mixed with concerns about undesirable consequences. Most people view science as instrumental in achieving important social goals, yet in a 1976 survey, only a small majority (52 percent) of respondents said they believed that science and technology have produced more good than harm. By far the greatest benefits perceived were in the field of medicine (81 percent). In other areas — improved living conditions, environmental conservation, energy programs and communication — science and technology were considered beneficial only 10-14 percent of the time. A review of logitudinal data on the public's confidence in people who run institutions found that the proportion of respondents who expressed "a great deal of confidence" in the scientific community declined from 56 percent to 43 percent between 1966 and 1976.[4] However, while regard for scientists declined in absolute terms, this mainly reflects the declining trust in most major institutions.[5] In this respect, scientists have fared rather well; in gauging the public's esteem for science relative to other occupations, science ranked only second behind medicine.

An important but often neglected point revealed by attitude surveys relates to the question of public control. People are clearly more worried about the impact of technology than about science, but when asked whether it is more important for society to control science or technology, 59 percent responded that both must be controlled equally and only 20 percent felt that neither should be controlled at all.[6] Science, this suggests, is regarded as a "normal" policy area, that is, an area open to political debate, and subject to public control.

This view is expressed more explicitly in many recent controversies over science.[7] Activities such as fetal research, in vitro fertilization, or the creation of new micro-organisms through recombinant DNA techniques are perceived by many people as changing the normal state of nature, violating cherished values, or altering the genetic structure of man. Socially accepted limits have not established for these research activities, so opposition crystalizes around particular applications of research and attempts are made on a case-by-case basis to define limits through administrative appeals or, increasingly, through litigation.

The issues at stake in such disputes have little to do with scientific merit. They bring to the evaluation of science notions of pluralism, of equity, of democratic participation — all characteristic of the political culture but quite at odds with beliefs held by scientists themselves.[8] And they express the kind of conflicting social judgments that surround any area of public policy. Is the creation of embryos through in vitro fertilization a boon for sterile women or is it a kind of manipulation that violates the sanctity of life? Is research into the genetic basis of criminal behavior a humane way to ameliorate problems of violence or is it a way to facilitate social control? Is fetal research a harmless technique that may contribute to medically useful knowledge or is it a violation of basic moral values?

Such disputes also engage scientists in open political debate, thereby challenging the very image of science as a neutral, apolitical activity that has allowed the development of a research system with minimal external control. This inevitably evokes a fearful response. At the 1978 Nobel Symposium on the ethics of science policy, a biologist expressed his fear that controversies would place scientists on the defensive and bureaucratize their activities, and, further, that this would discourage bright, young people from entering the field. He warned against "DNA hysteria" and argued that "a public prematurely exposed to technical discussions will lead to the growth of an onerous bureaucracy and regulations that will hamper scientific advance."[9] Similarly, a recent editorial in Science argued against regulation: "Informed consent may be hazardous to health"; some suggest that such external controls would virtually paralyze the research process.

At the same time, more and more scientists are aware of the inherent difficulty of distinguishing science from ethical considerations. For example, Baruch Blumberg has observed that biological knowledge can bring about serious conflicts between public health interests and individual liberty. These are precisely the kinds of conflicts that classically have led to calls for regulations.[10]

What, in fact, is the impact of all this brouhaha on science policy? Do disputes directly affect research funding? Have demands for greater participation significantly changed decision-making procedures? How have conflict and the demands for greater public scrutiny actually affected research? Answers to these questions, just like answers to those about the significance of any political trend, must necessarily be speculative. However, by assembling information in a variety of areas, certain patterns emerge that can guide a tentative analysis.

The Impact of Disputes on Research Support

In 1977, Pierre Soupart applied to NIH for renewal of his grant for research on *in vitro* fertilization. He had been doing research in this area for more than a decade, but in 1975 public opposition to such research had led to a *de facto* moratorium on federal funding. Soupart's proposal was approved on the basis of its scientific merit and then forwarded to HEW's Ethics Advisory Board. Meanwhile, Louise Brown* was born, accelerating a public controversy over the ethical implications of *in vitro* fertilization. Sensitive to the growing debate, then-Secretary of HEW Joseph Califano asked the Advisory Board to broaden its consideration of Soupart's application to include the scientific, ethical, legal, and social issues broadly associated with this technique.[11] While the Board deliberated, funding delays became inevitable and research took place only in privately-financed facilities.

In some cases, research funding has actually been withdrawn from a project as a direct consequence of protest. One such project was the Center for the Study of the Reduction of Violence at UCLA, organized to study the origins of pathologically-violent behavior, to identify violent predispositions, and to develop techniques for treatment of criminal offenders. This interdisciplinary center was to conduct research in pharmaceutical, biological, and social sciences; its research program included a spectrum of studies ranging from basic to applied and from experimental to therapeutic research. The researchers viewed their work as a public service — a use of science to seek humane solutions to a difficult social problem. Funding was approved by the California Department of Mental Hygiene and the federal Law Enforcement Assistance Administration. But then critics of this research reacted strongly. They argued that, in such studies, the use of human subjects would be coercive and that the research itself would encourage pernicious mechanisms for social control. In 1974, after a year of conflict, all promises for research support were withdrawn.[12]

Clearly public opposition to research can result in a denial of funding. But such constraints also may never materialize. Worries about the impact of public criticism of support for recombinant DNA research were unwarranted. NIH supported 207 projects using this technique in

---

*She was the first "test-tube" baby.

May 1977, and 560 in September 1978. Scientists have flocked to this field and it has been argued that the DNA controversy, by expanding communication among scientists, actually accelerated growth in the field.[13]

This is not to imply that political and social values are irrelevant to the public support of science. On the contrary, there are many examples to suggest the importance of political criteria. The National Science Foundation (NSF) was long reluctant to fund the social sciences. NSF documents and public hearings include many statements of concern about the controversial political connotations of social science, and the possibility that these would undermine confidence in other scientific activities. When the Foundation finally did fund the social sciences, it was careful to support only "ultra-safe lines of inquiry."[14]* In another area, federal legislation prevents the use of public monies for any research dealing with a U.S. surrender. This law was passed after a social scientist wrote a politically controversial book (supported by federal funds) about the fallacy of expecting unconditional surrender in the international context of a nuclear age.

The point is not to minimize the importance of political values in setting priorities, but to emphasize that, in the absence of an overall science policy, public reaction to specific research practices affects research support only when someone with decision-making power is listening. That is, the impact of opposition depends upon whose political values are reflected in research decisions; on how the system of control is organized; and on where the power lies. These questions of control are thus the major issues in disputes over science.

Impact of Disputes on Decision-Making Institutions

One major and important effect of the proliferation of controversies over science has been the search for decision-making procedures that would better incorporate social values into the research process. The number of new commissions, review boards, committees, and panels devoted to the assessment of science is remarkable. Most include lay numbers on the assumption that representing a wider range of interests in the decision-making process will restore public confidence in science and defuse protest. However, the influence of lay participants is questionable, for the structure of most institutional experiments reflects a basic contradiction between the norms of the political culture and the expectations among scientists of self-regulation and internal control.

In 1969, then-Senator Walter Mondale introduced legislation to create a national advisory commission to study the ethical, social and legal implications of biomedical science. Nothing happened at that time, but in 1974 Senator Edward Kennedy introduced a modified version of this legislation as part of the National Research Act, thereby establishing the National Commission for the Protection of Human Subjects of Biomedical and Behavioral Research. The original structure of

---

*NSF support of social science research was dramatically curtailed by the initial budget decisions of the Reagan Administration.

this Commission reflected the assumption that non-scientific input into research policy was useful and necessary.[15] Of the eleven commissioners, no more than five could be engaged in biomedical or behavioral research. The Commission's purpose was to identify the ethical principles that should underly research in human subjects and to recommend guidelines and appropriate regulations for research to the Secretary of HEW.

When its statutory term was completed in October 1978, the Commission was replaced by a Presidential Commission for the Study of Ethical Problems in Medicine and Biomedical Behavior Research, budgeted at five million dollars annually and given a jurisdiction encompassing all Federal agencies (even the CIA). Responding to the growing number and scope of disputes over biomedical and behavioral research, this Commission has a far broader mandate — to study requirements for informed consent, the definition of death, the questions raised by genetic testing and counseling, the distribution of health services, the problems of confidentiality, and "any other appropriate matters" all within four years.[16] Its eleven Commissioners include six who are engaged in biomedical or behavioral research or medical practice. The other five are from fields of ethics, law, government or other sciences. The composition of this group seems to reflect the need to open membership to a broader range of scientists and professionals, but it puts less emphasis on non-scientific involvement than its predecessor, despite its very broad concern with social and ethical issues.

The Institutional Review Boards established by the Department of Health and Human Services and the Public Health Service to review the adequacy of safeguards to protect human subjects at the local institutional level are organized so as to increase public accountability but without impeding research. A survey organized by the National Commission on Research found that 50 percent of IRB members were biomedical scientists, 21 percent were social scientists and the rest were non-scientists (including administrators, lawyers, and clergymen).[17] The study suggests that the scientists on these boards have a dominant influence and that there is little indication that IRB's have significantly obstructed research. Several proposals have called for more lay members on these Boards and for meetings that would be open to public scrutiny, but to date responsibility for monitoring and evaluating actual research practice remains with the researcher.

The recombinant DNA dispute generated a proposal for a national commission in the area of genetics research. This never materialized, but the controversy did result in several additional layers in the NIH decision-making procedures. In 1974, NIH formed a Recombinant DNA Molecule Program Advisory Committee as a technical group of rather limited scope. Criticized for its narrow view, NIH convened a Director's Advisory Committee to allow both scientists and the public to comment on proposed guidelines. This committee was more broadly constituted; its 25 members include several lawyers and ethicists, plus several non-scientists who had been critical of the existing controls over DNA research. While the committee has held some open meetings, critics continue to feel that its efforts to include public input are inadequate.[18]

NIH also developed a multi-level committee structure to oversee individual projects and required the creation of local biohazards committees in all institutions undertaking recombinant DNA research.

This active research area stimulated other efforts to increase local
influence on research decisions, such as the citizen review boards in
Cambridge, and in a number of other university communities. Finally,
the controversy generated a series of aborted efforts to establish Congressional control over this research area. Despite the broad-ranging
value concerns that made recombinant DNA research the focus of extended conflict, all of these boards and committees confined their
deliberations to the relatively manageable problem of risk. They gave
little attention to more difficult questions concerning the potential
abuse of this research or to the broader problems associated with
genetic manipulation, and this has made these procedures vulnerable to
persistent criticism.

The controversy over *in vitro* fertilization also changed decision-
making procedures, but here again careful selection of members on an
advisory committee assured scientific control. The HEW Ethics Advisory Board, which was intended to set the framework for future regulation and practice in this area, had 13 members, seven of whom were
scientists and physicians. After a series of public hearings throughout
the country, the Board concluded in favor of continuing this research,
although with qualifications requiring that research comply with the
guidelines governing human experimentation and that embryos be sustained for no more than 14 days. As in the recombinant DNA case, this
Board has been criticized for emphasizing problems of risk, and for side-
stepping many of the difficult value issues that made such research controversial. The decision avoided obstructing research, but it has not
satisfied the opposition.[19]

In addition, disputes have generated proposals to encourage greater
democratization of research decisions, better public access to information, and a more adequate distribution of expertise. Programs such as
the NSF "Science for Citizens" effort and a variety of public education
projects have resulted. However, most institutional changes provide only a veneer of participation. The complex and esoteric nature of many
decisions concerning science, the very real difficulty in coming to grips
with ethical issues, and the continued faith in science as a solution to
social problems have left control of the research system firmly within
the scientific community.

Impact of Disputes on Regulation of Research

Has the struggle for control of research actually resulted in obstruc-
tive regulation? Again, let us look at some specific cases.

In the dispute surrounding *in vitro* fertilization, the Ethics Advisory
Board eventually approved the conduct of research, and scientists work-
ing in this field observed that its qualifications were reasonable. Indeed,
Soupart's research already complied with the Board's requirements.

Similarly, the NIH guidelines for recombinant DNA research
established biological and physical containment requirements that

many scientists considered as reasonably unobstructive. Even these have gradually been relaxed, and the Advisory Committee has recommended exempting about 80-85 percent of the studies from federal guidelines. The local citizen review boards, a source of deep concern as they sought to assess recombinant DNA guidelines, all supported a continuation of the research and accepted the premises of the scientific community about the value of this work. Lay involvement in NIH advisory boards did not destroy the peer-review system; study sections continue to control the quality and direction of research.

The prolonged dispute over fetal research, intensified by its relationship to the controversial abortion issue, threatened to result in restrictions. Indeed, the deliberation over the ethical problems involved in this research did result in an eight-month moratorium. However, the HEW Guidelines of 1975 basically accepted the importance of this research and the scientific reasoning which lay behind the controversial experiments. These guidelines rejected the moral restrictions that had been demanded by critics. Experiments that met the requirements of scientific merit and social worth were allowed, and in this case scientists won a substantive victory over their critics.[20]

Constraints have been placed on experimentation on prisoners and other vulnerable groups, but these requirements can hardly be interpreted as an effort to limit scientific inquiry. One survey of 2,000 researchers and 800 IRB members concluded that the IRBs often require some modification of proposals, but that outright rejection of a proposal is rare. While half of the researchers interviewed felt that their research had been impeded in some way, only eight percent felt that such difficulties had outweighed the benefits of this review procedure.[21] Most responded that the IRB judgments were sound and indeed in many cases had improved their research. In effect, the IRBs originally established to control research on human subjects have mainly been preoccupied with the consent form and the question of whether consent procedures offer adequate legal protection of the researcher and his situation.

A current debate focuses on the extension of the Freedom of Information Act that would disclose research proposals and research findings prior to completion. Concerned that access to data from clinical trials before their statistical significance was established would bias research, NIH turned to the Ethics Advisory Board. This Board has recommended that research be exempt from the Act.

Similarly, the National Commission for the Protection of Human Subjects recommended that proposals be publicly available only after they were funded, so as to protect patent rights and preserve the competitive spirit of science.

Interpretations

Growing public concern about the control of research expressed in the confrontations and protests of the 1970's reflects changes both in the constituency of science and in science itself.

The constituency of science has clearly broadened, reflecting in part a perception that science is a social problem. Evidence for this expanding interest is clear in the proliferation of popular science journals; even *Penthouse* is publishing a science magazine. An expanded constituency is a sign of health, but it also creates an "attentive public" not only passively curious about science but also actively concerned about its effects. Public concerns reflect some non-trivial changes, both in science and its applications.

First, as Steven Muller has noted in his paper in this volume, scientific research no longer fits the "Einstein image" of the rumpled genius standing before a blackboard. It depends on sophisticated and very costly technology and large teams of scientists. "Proven ability to generate grant support" is increasingly stated as a requirement in advertisements for scientific personnel, in effect setting new professional standards that recognize the dependence of the scientific enterprise on federal funds.[22] Science, in this context, competes in the political arena with other national priorities.

Second, the scope of the research and its application have broadened. The tendency of scientists to claim extensive territory for the concepts and tools of their disciplines and, in particular, the extension of concepts in the biological sciences to generalizations about human behavior, is bound to be controversial. The very relevance of science to social problems, the use of science to justify other policy decisions, and science's increased role in public affairs have destroyed the conventional distinction between science and technology. As the production of knowledge and its application become irreversibly linked, greater political direction is inevitable.

Third, the techniques of research have become more sophisticated, thus increasing the risks to research subjects and creating the very significant power to manipulate human life. The intrusion of science and technology is real, affecting more and more people and inevitably subjecting science to critical scrutiny.

Fourth, in the prevailing social climate, activities once acceptable because of the priority placed on scientific progress are now challenged. In the post-Sputnik years, it would have been difficult to imagine a serious discussion about the limits to inquiry. But the ideology of progress has given way to an ideology of limits, and questions of ethics enter the evaluation of science, just as they enter the assessment of other social and political activities.

Finally, the scientific community inevitably shares in the general breakdown in society of the legitimacy of constituted authority. Greater public participation and accountability are pervasive themes in all policy areas, as confidence in administrative and political structures declines. Alisdair MacIntyre has argued that regulation is a substitute for morality. "Resort to the law is a sign that deeper moral relationships have broken down."[23] Individual responsibility, he argues, is "an endangered concept." No community is given full discretion, and scientists are no exception.

Scientists have, however, come out rather well. Although faced with demands for greater accountability and a swell of public criticism, power over the research system remains within the scientific community. While red tape and paper work have certainly increased, few of the recent institutional changes have imposed significant limits on scientific inquiry or obstructed scientific progress.

To date the pattern is clear; scientists have been able to control the regulatory process much as industry learned to manage regulation — for its own ends. Yet, the very concept of external constraints continues to provoke a defensive response from the scientific community. As in other social systems, scientists seek to control their territory. They try to negotiate space in which they can maintain their autonomy and their image as a self-governing community:

- "External regulation is for technological application, not for scientific research;"[24]
- "Ethical decisions are best made by scientists who understand the value implications of their decisions."[25]

The 1970's were a decade of concern about the social and ethical implications of science, a decade marked by demands for increased accountability and for greater public control. These demands have called attention to the public character of scientific research and to the need of setting priorities that reflect the public will. Neils Bohr once remarked that forecasting is difficult, especially about the future; even so, it seems reasonable to suggest that the 1980's will be a period of intense negotiation in establishing these priorities and in evolving political relationships that are appropriate both in the context of new developments in science and in new applications of research.

REFERENCES

1. Don Price, "The Scientific Establishment," *Science,* August 18, 1961, p. 1099.

2. National Commission on Research, "Accountability: Resolving the Morality of the Partnership," *Science,* March 14, 1980, pp. 1177-82.

3. Donald Frederickson, "A Scientist's View of Priorities and Control of the Organization of Research," in T. Segerstedt, ed., *Ethics for Science Policy,* (New York: Pergamon Press for the Royal Swedish Academy of Sciences, 1979) pp. 81-89.

4. The above data on public attitudes are from the National Science Board, *Science Indicators 1976,* p. 168-182. Similar ambivalence shows up in European surveys. See Commission of the European Communities, *Science and European Public Opinion,* Brussels, 1977. A more recent survey, focusing specifically on medical research, shows greater confidence in this field than others. Most respondents felt medical research has changed life for the better (very much better — 59%, somewhat for the better — 34%). But 49% agreed that in deciding what to do, scientists are more concerned with their own research interests than with public benefits; National Commission for the Protection of Human Subjects, *Special Study,* DHEW Publication No. (OS) 78-0015, 1978.

5. Between 1966 and 1976 those expressing a great deal of confidence in Congress declined from 42% to 14%; in the heads of major corporations from 55% to 35%; and in educators from 61% to 37%.

6. Opinion Research Corporation, *Attitudes of the U.S. Public Towards Science and Technology,* Study III, September 1976, p. 51.

7. For a review and analysis of these conflicts, see Dorothy Nelkin, ed., *Controversy: Politics of Technical Decisions,* (Beverly Hills: Sage Publications, 1979).

8. Everett Mendelsohn and Peter Weingart, "The Social Assessment of Science: Issues and Perspectives," in E. Mendelsohn, D. Nelkin, and P. Weingart, eds., *The Social Assessment of Science,* Conference Proceedings, University of Bielefeld, 1978.

9. Bernard Davis, "Limits in the Regulation of Scientific Research," in T. Segerstedt, *op. cit.,* pp. 203-214.

10. Baruch Blumberg, "Bioethical Questions Related to Hepatitus B Antigen," *Americal Journal of Clinical Pathology,* 65, May 5, 1976, p. 84ff.

11. See LeRoy Walters, "Human *In Vitro* Fertilization: A Review of the Ethical Literature," *Hastings Center Report* 9, August 4, 1979, pp. 23-43.

12. Dorothy Nelkin and Judith Swazey, "Science and Social Control: Controversies over Research on Violence," in Hastings Center, *The Dynamics of Scientific Research* (forthcoming).

13. Charles Wiener, "Historical Perspectives on the Recombinant DNA Controversy," in J. Morgan and W. Wheelan, eds., *Recombinant DNA and Genetic Experimentation,* (New York: Pergamon Press, 1979).

14. Science Policy Research Division, Library of Congress, *Technical Information for Congress,* April 25, 1969, p. 103.

15. See *National Research Act,* P.L. 93-34.

16. George Annas, "All the President's Bioethics," *Hastings Center Report,* February 1979, pp. 14-15. Also see Public Law 95-622, November 9, 1978.

17. Study by Bradford Gray for the National Commission for the Protection of Human Subjects, *Reports and Recommendations on Institutional Review Boards,* DHEW OS 78-0008, September 1978.

18. See discussion in Sheldon Krimsky, "Regulating Recombinant DNA Research," in D. Nelkin, ed., *Controversy, op. cit.,* pp. 227-253.

19. See critique of the EAB by Margaret O'Brien Steinfels, "Ethics Advisory Board and *In Vitro* Fertilization," *Hastings Center Report,* 9, June 3, 1979, pp. 5-9.

20. Steven Maynard-Moody, "The Fetal Research Dispute," in Nelkin, ed., *Controversy, op. cit.,* pp. 197-212.

21. Bradford Gray and Robert Cooke, "The Impact of Institutional Review Boards on Research," *Hastings Center Report,* 10, February 1, 1980, pp. 36-41.

22. See Letter to the Editor in *Physics Today,* April 1980, p. 15.

23. Alisdair MacIntyre, "Regulation: A Substitute for Morality," *Hastings Center Report,* 10, February 1, 1980, pp. 31-33.

24. Bernard Davis, *op. cit.*

25. Edward Diener and Rich Candrell, *Ethics in Social and Behavioral Research,* (Chicago: University of Chicago Press, 1978), p. 5. For discussion of this tension in the social sciences see Dorothy Nelkin, "Limits to Social Science Inquiry," in T. Beauchamp, *Ethics in Social Sciences* (forthcoming).

Basic Research on The Campus:
A University View

Steven Muller

The United States is now at a critical juncture with respect to the future of basic research. Furthermore, American research universities are inextricably involved since over 70 percent of all basic research done in the United States is carried on within universities. This situation is somewhat unusual within the international context; in many other highly developed industrial states, much basic research is done by non-university organizations uniquely charged with this mission, such as institutes of national academies of science, or the Max Planck Institutes of the Federal Republic of Germany. Even in the international context, however, commercial industry concentrates primarily on applied research and does relatively little basic research. The ingredients of what now must be called — without hyperbole — a crisis in the United States can be identified by the following questions:

1. Will sufficient federal funds continue to be available to support a significant volume of basic research?
2. Will American universities continue to be able to carry out basic research on campuses on the basis of present patterns of funding?
3. If federal funding is sufficiently available but universities cease being able to respond, can new institutions for the conduct of basic research evolve?
4. If major American universities surrender much of their basic research mission, what kinds of institutions will they become?

Much has been said and written recently about the adversarial relationship between the federal government and the major American research universities. Most of the attention has focused on the government's role in attaching new and onerous conditions to the support it provides to universities for basic research. There are grave problems involved here, but these matters are only the tip of the iceberg. The fundamental problem is that basic research has become such a large-scale and expensive activity as to constitute a heavy drain on federal budgets, and an intolerable financial burden on the American university. Basically, the problem is money. If sound decisions are to emerge at this

Steven Muller is President of The Johns Hopkins University.

critical juncture, the financial problem which has produced it must be clearly understood and then resolved.

In 1979, the celebration of the centennial birthday of Albert Einstein produced countless reproductions of the rumpled genius standing before a blackboard filled with scribbles in chalk. Leaving tributes to Einstein aside, this image probably reinforced the popular myth that basic research involves primarily the solitary mind engaged in hard thought. Actually, and to a much greater extent than the public understands, the facts are radically different. During the past three or four decades, basic research has become wholly dependent upon sophisticated technology which has vastly enlarged its scope but even more vastly increased its costs. While the human mind obviously still dominates the research process, less and less basic research is carried on by single individuals, and more and more is necessarily done by ever larger teams of people working together.

Complicated calculations are no longer done in someone's head but by computers, which also store the data once kept in notebooks or on scraps of paper. For example, most of physics now involves huge arrays of instrumentation that demand platoons of talent for operation, and regiments of talent for maintenance. Many of these instruments are so large that they can only be constructed once or twice, then to be used in common by national as well as international teams. Though less widely understood, an equivalent explosion of instrumentation has been evolving in the other physical and natural sciences as well. Chemistry laboratories may still have their traditional beakers and smells, but they also depend on electron microscopes and nuclear magnetic resonance spectrometers. Biological and health research is equally dependent on lasers, nuclear accelerators, and electronic scanners.

Increasingly, advanced work in these fields requires interdisciplinary talent, and a huge fraction of time and effort must be devoted to the maintenance and adaptation of huge, complicated and expensive instruments so that research may be advanced. This situation is more acute in physics and natural science, but the social sciences have also become increasingly dependent on computers and microprocessors, and even the humanities have been affected.

What all this means is that the support of basic research now necessarily involves billions of dollars, for which the federal government is virtually the sole source. It is only natural that such huge annual expenditures should be questioned and evaluated in light of a host of other pressing national priorities. Billion dollar appropriations for ventures into space, or devoted to lead shielded chambers filled with multi-million dollar equipment for cancer research or genetic experimentation, have their own recognized merit and excitement. But these expenditures compete with everything from Social Security to urban decay and environmental protection or national defense. It is understandable that there are doubts concerning the public's determination to continue to spend ever-increasing billions of dollars on basic research. What is equally clear is that the option of doing basic research on the cheap no longer exists. Costs will rise inexorably, and if adequate appropriations are not made, the result will be an unavoidable decline in the quality and progress of basic research.

From the perspective of the university, the problem is more stark. This is because choice has all but disappeared. Basic research, quite simply, has become so expensive that no university can execute it on any significant scale with its own resources. Worse than that, universities are no longer even in a position to do so on the traditional basis of cost sharing, on which their receipt of federal funds for basic research has been based since the end of World War II. While individual researchers are scattered in colleges and universities throughout the United States, the evolution in the scale and cost of basic research long ago created a situation in which the overwhelming bulk of basic research is carried on in only a tiny minority of this country's 3,300 institutions of higher education. Perhaps a hundred campuses can lay claim to being major research institutions, and in truth less than 50 or 60 produce high-quality basic research in large volume. The plain fact is that these institutions can no longer afford to subsidize basic research activities adequately with their own resources, even if unlimited federal support were available but awarded according to present patterns.

It was fair enough years ago for the government to assume that universities wanted to make commitments of their own to do basic research, in large part because basic research properly continues to be regarded as an inextricable part of the university's teaching mission. In fact, training of young scientists remains absolutely dependent upon their involvement in basic research. Basic research equally depends for its execution on these same young scientists, even if they cut their teeth in the laboratory as junior members of a large team whose initial effort is devoted mostly to learning the uses and maintenance of instrumentation. However, when the university's share of supporting basic research runs annually into the millions of dollars, cost sharing becomes an impossibility. Universities have become unable to muster the necessary funds from state appropriations, private endowments, tuition income, or private gifts. Thus they are deprived of choice. Either the federal government assumes a larger burden, or the work quite simply cannot be afforded. More than anything else, this quandary accounts for the sometimes shrill tone one hears from the campuses.

A rational solution is possible but it will be difficult to achieve. What it will require, primarily, is a fundamental readjustment of the traditional partnership in basic research between the federal government and the nation's major research universities. It would not be rational for the government to attempt to shift basic research away from the university community. For the government, any such effort would involve a multi-billion dollar investment in new facilities, to replace those which already exist at enormous expense on the major research campuses. For the major research university it would spell the loss of top talent, which presumably would move right along with the moving of federal funds. For both government and university, a horrendous new problem would exist with respect to the nurturing of young scientific talent. Without the basic research mission, universities would no longer be able to effectively train such talent. An attempt by government to shift such training to non-university institutions, devoted to basic research, would achieve nothing less than the creation of a whole new set of academic institutions.

One may also rule out as an alternative any substantial shift of the burden of supporting basic research to the private sector of the American economy. While it would be part of any rational solution to expect private industry to play a greater role in the sponsorship of basic research, the total dollar volume involved simply rules out private industry as an alternative to federal sponsorship. The only thing that makes sense is for the federal government to continue to look to the major research universities for the bulk of the nation's basic research effort, and to provide funding for this purpose.

Such funding would have to be permanent and substantial, quite apart from the arguments about limits to government control that would adversely affect academic integrity, or the need of universities to provide scrupulous accountability for the use of federal funds. In effect, the federal government would have to give explicit recognition to the obvious fact that a relatively small group of major research universities already constitute the resource base for most basic research, and that they need to be identified as national research institutions for this purpose.

Not all of these universities are alike, and some effort will be required to be selective in terms of quality and as fair as possible in geographic distribution. One possible way to proceed would be to segment basic research into several major categories, and to establish national resource centers at institutions already strong in a particular segment of basic science. A hypothetical west-coast institution might then, for example, qualify as a national resource center in biological science and in basic engineering, while a mid-western institution would qualify in physical science and basic engineering, and yet another mythical eastern institution in the biological sciences and in basic engineering. The really important factor would be a durable federal commitment to assume the full burden of basic research at such prospective centers on university campuses, which would entail funding equivalent to endowment support in addition to annual grants.

This, of course, is not really a farfetched notion. When the federal government awards grants for building construction or large-scale instrumentation, the effect is already that of a permanent commitment. What needs to be added is an equivalent permanent funding for the maintenance of the facility, the maintenance and replacement of equipment, and core operating personnel. Whether this is done best in the long term by federal ownership of the facilities and equipment and a lease to the university, or by continued direct grants to the institutions is subject to argument. Permanent funding for core personnel, however, is not likely to be handled effectively by stationing federal personnel on campus. Here the traditional model of providing funding to the institution to recruit and deploy the personnel seems to be the only viable approach. The required difference would be the need for a permanent grant to enable the university to do so. This in turn requires recognition that education in advanced science is an inextricable part of the basic research mission.

At least two other changes in present modes of operation would also be required. The post-World War II legacy of denying to universities the opportunity to charge the costs of independent research and development as a direct cost of basic research must be abandoned. Industrial research and development (IR&D) costs have consistently been allowable to all of the government's industrial contractors, while denied to universities. This is not only unfair but counterproductive.

An interesting illustration of what is involved here may be found at The Johns Hopkins University. On the teaching campuses of this institution, no IR&D costs can be charged to the federal government, and as a result almost no IR&D is in prospect for the future because of the lack of available university funds. At the Applied Physics Laboratory of The Johns Hopkins University, which constitutes a geographically separate non-teaching campus and which contracts directly with the federal government as a non-academic part of the university, IR&D has consistently been a legitimate charge on government contracts, and has evolved into a multi-million dollar enterprise from which have sprung almost all of the major research advances developed at the laboratory. The assumption that major research universities can and should provide their own funding for independent research and development now flies in the face of the financial condition under which these universities operate, regardless of whether they function in the private sector or as state institutions.

The second indispensable change involves the calculation of the allowable indirect costs of research. The traditional guidelines here, recently reinforced by a much-discussed and still controversial set of changes, attempt too rigid a confinement of indirect costs to the narrowest possible fallout from direct costs. What is required is a clearer recognition by government that the basic research mission is inseparably part of the university's total mission. A more rational and comprehensive recalculation of indirect costs is needed, particularly in the area of supporting the student participation which is so insolubly part of the training for future talent.

In summary, the future of American basic research is currently at stake. Much more needs to be done to persuade the American people that the ever-rising costs are worth paying. But even if continued investment by the federal government in the funding of basic research remains a national priority, new measures must be taken to enable major American research universities to continue to be this country's principal resource for basic research. The volume and price of the enterprise have outrun the capacity of the university effectively to share the cost. The universities will have a difficult time in making the internal adjustments required to carry on the large-scale interdisciplinary basic research of the future. They cannot even make the necessary effort without new ways of funding.

Science, Government and Policy: A Four Decade Perspective

Emmanuel R. Piore

The Current Situation

Continuing discussion and action are taking place within several components of the federal government, in both the legislative and executive branches, concerning research performed at universities by contract or grants, with funds supplied by Washington. This debate involves such items as overhead, audit procedures, and faculty time. There is pressure from the government; in the university there is continuing concern about long-range stability and the desirability of peer review. The universities need stability and funds; the federal government desires improved "bookkeeping" and better records to assure the Congress and the electorate that funds made available are "properly" used. This is far from a complete list of concerns.

Usually the government's view prevails. The immediate consequence is an increase in the administrative staffs of both government and the university and such increases reduce the funds available for research. Right now this is occurring when there is general agreement that in order to increase the health of our society, it is important to reduce the "red tape" and regulations generated by the federal government.

Do all these auditing procedures and bookkeeping increase the quality of research? Or do they inhibit the spirit of free inquiry so necessary for progress in the sciences and, in particular, so vital in those areas of the sciences that are at the cutting edge of the unknown? The atmosphere in institutions dedicated to scientific contribution must be one that encourages the creative activity of individual scientists.

A recent incident may be relevant here. The Office of Management and Budget, in order to establish uniform procedures among several federal agencies that provide funds for research, proposed a time-keeping mechanism that would provide a direct measure of the time an investigation spends on research — a "time clock record." Only per-

Dr. Emmanuel R. Piore was involved in the development of post-World War II government-science relationships as a staff member of the Office of Naval Research, where he was Chief Scientist from 1951-55. He was with IBM from 1956 until his retirement in 1972, with his last position being Vice President and Chief Scientist. He was a member of the President's Science Advisory Committee and the National Science Board.

sonal action and perseverance by Saunders MacLane, Mason Distinguished Professor of Mathematics at University of Chicago, was able to modify the OMB point of view. His most telling argument was that this is not the way to encourage the creative ability of imaginative and talented scientists. In addition, MacLane argued, research is intimately coupled with the training of graduate students, a relationship between the master and the apprentice. The training of future scientists would have been eroded. The government's proposals would have changed the function of the professor.

This incident illustrates the current lack of definition in the relationship between government and science and the stresses in the system of federal support for science which have developed over the past few years. In order to understand the current situation fully, it is necessary to look back over almost four decades.

Development of Government-Science Relations

Federal agencies have available, and use, a number of institutional mechanisms to support academic research. Some do not involve universities directly. In 1945, the federal government made an implicit commitment to support academic science.

Life was simple once. During the past 35 years, as funds have increased and as the number of researchers has increased, life has become more complex. At times the purpose of the original thrust and national policy has been has become unfocused or even forgotten.

Between 1945 and 1950 Congress created the Office of Naval Research, the National Science Foundation, the Atomic Energy Commission, and the National Institutes of Health. The preambles in the legislative action creating these agencies all contain broad statements bearing directly on national science policy. The backdrop of this legislation was Vannevar Bush's report *The Endless Frontier* and the follow-up report by John Steelman of the Bureau of the Budget. Both reports emphasized the importance of science to this nation, both culturally and economically.*

The flow of money for science is controlled both by the Office of Management and Budget and by the authorization and appropriations committees of both houses of Congress. Their actions have a significant impact on which fields of science will be supported; in addition, their actions determine the health of science within the various fields. Apart from these appropriations of money, there are also operational components that implicitly modify national science policy. National science policy is profoundly affected by controls imposed by the Office

---

*It is interesting to remember that the legislation creating the National Science Foundation was a test of political strength between President Truman and Vannevar Bush. Bush hoped to untie the Foundation from the normal administrative control of the President and Congress, thereby giving it the freedom that the Smithsonian Institute had and creating an entity more in the tradition of a private foundation. Truman obviously won. In time, the Director of the Foundation became an agent of the White House, and thus lost independent responsibility for the health of science.

of Management and Budget, by procedures of the Executive departments and agencies which dispense the funds appropriated to them, by the administrative structures and procedures generated internally in academia, and let us not forget — by Congressional legislation.

In all the discussions, surrounding the decision-making process, very little consideration, evaluation, or judgment is given as to whether the performance of a scientist is improved or inhibited, whether the creative ability of the scientist is endangered, or whether the "red tape" generated is good or bad for science.

Historically, the first articulation of science policy in the western world came from royal decree in the last half of the seventeenth century, with the creation of institutions such as the Royal Society of London, a comparable society in France and other European countries. In this country the American Philosophical Society was created in 1740; its charter is typical of the European royal societies charters: "... for promotion of useful knowledge among the British plantations ..." In each of these charters the welfare of the nation was coupled with progress in science. These charters symbolized the recognition of the scientific community by government and our current generation does not challenge this observation.

The societies became institutionalized within two or three centuries. They all had specific operational policies. For example, each had a corresponding secretary, or some other means, to communicate the scientific advancements or results of great moment. Gradually, the communications or letters were replaced with an orderly publication, scientific journal, or transaction. This tradition has a contemporary counterpart: the government has assumed the responsibility for some of the cost of publication in learned journals. Thus one of the operational policies which has been consistent historically is publication; another is the sharing of research conclusions with the world. Thus science is independent of national boundaries; in fact, it was identified very early as an international activity.

During World War II scientists left research and engaged in the development of new weapons, drugs, and the like. Many universities made their facilities available for this work and graduate instruction in the sciences and in engineering was greatly reduced. In the traditional sense, there was very little basic scientific activity during the war.

At the end of the war, there was a general move to provide support to science, and to enable scientists to return to their laboratories and to their traditional activity, basic research. Funds were made available by the Army, the Navy, and the Manhattan District for such purposes. Congress, having created the Office of Naval Research, the R&D Division in the Army, AEC, the National Institutes of Health, and NSF, supported the expenditure of funds.

These legislative actions set the following policy: each executive department and agency whose mission depended on "technology" and analysis had the "right" or responsibility to do or support research which was basic in character. No federal agency was given the single authority to support science; no group in Washington had a monopoly on research support.

Mechanisms for Support of Science

The support supplied by the agencies mentioned above between 1945 and early 1950 falls into five categories which still operate today. The support funded 1. the construction of large facilities operated by a consortium of universities; 2. large laboratories in academia where the actual research undertaken was determined by and carried out under control of a laboratory director; 3. the acquisition of specialized equipment; 4. funding for unique institutions; and 5. funding of individual investigators.

A leading example in the first category was Brookhaven National Laboratory on Long Island. In 1945, the future of existing laboratories under the control of the Manhattan District — Los Alamos, Oak Ridge, Stanford, Argonne — was not clear. There was a need for a large particle accelerator for unclassified research. Nine eastern universities created a not-for-profit corporation; on the west coast, there was what is now called the Lawrence Radiation Laboratory. Potential academic users were able to determine their research programs without any direct intervention by the government. A managing corporation composed of a group of universities set a pattern which is evident today in the Fermi Laboratory. Still another example of this is the consortium of universities which operate the main astronomical observatories, such as the National Center for Atmospheric Research in Boulder. In all of these laboratories, there is competition for excellence.

The two most important issues in such institutions are who selects the director and how the research program is determined. Significantly, neither issue is resolved in Washington. As a rule these laboratories have large and mostly instruments. The instruments themselves, large or small, set the pace for the advancement of science.

The conversion of the NDRC/OSRD group from war to peace, and the creation of new groups whose members had made important technical contributions during the war years, resulted in the establishment of large university laboratories such as MIT's Research Lab in Electronics, and similar groups at Columbia, Harvard, and Stanford. The universities were responsible for selecting the staff, the director, and the program which was reviewed once a year during a site visit by government program officers.

At this point in our history, block grants for supporting these large labs have gone out of style. The shift came primarily from individual scientists. Their notion was simple. The amount of money available through peer review was reduced as long as block grants were popular. In addition, those awarding block grants never considered, or debated, either the quality of the science or the amount of red tape involved.

The importance of instruments to the progress in various fields of science was stressed earlier. One example of this occurred in cryogenic, low temperature physics, including superconductivity and superfluidity. During the 1940's, a comparatively inexpensive helium liquifier had been developed. About a dozen or so of these liquifiers were made available through government support to various researchers. There was no problem identifying who in the scientific world could utilize such equipment profitably, i.e. profitably in scientific terms. A second example of scientific instruments was the Linear Electronic Accelerator. Again, there was general agreement as to who had the talent; the only group in the country that had the necessary capability was at Stanford. No peer review was required. The participants' contribution during the war made such identification easy.

A third, and unsuccessful, example was the radar systems which were no longer useful in the Defense Department. They were made available to engineers so that they could enter radio astronomy research. This support did not work; it was terminated in a year or a year and a half. The idea was premature. Proficiency in technology does not necessarily create enough understanding of a scientific field to enable investigators to make real use of a newly available technological capability.

During the post-war period, unique institutions such as the Scripps and the Woods Hole Oceanographic Institutions were also given block grants. They had the critical skills and it was agreed that it was in the national interest for such institutions to grow in size and competence.

Depending on the scientific discipline and in some measure on the knowledge and respect a granting officer had among his scientific constituency, peer review became the mechanism of choice for allocating funds to individual investigators. A great deal depended on the tradition of the particular scientific field since the granting officer was aware of both individual work and contribution during the war. When sums were small and the applicants were young and large in number, the selection of awardees was delegated to committees in the National Research Council.

Impact of Changes over the Past Three Decades

In reviewing the operational policies and administrative procedures for the support of science, it is well to observe that times have changed in terms of funds, money, and the size of the academic scientific effort. When the original relationship between government and science began, everything was small both in government and academia.

During those early days, the granting officer, whether he utilized a peer review mechanism or not, made an individual commitment that his choice was sound, and the program or project selected would succeed. Thus internally, within the governmental agencies, he was involved in the administrative procedure imposed by government auditors and accountants. Any problem that came to light that was annoying to the research performance could be resolved by the granting officer internally. In addition, the granting officer's judgment was visible to the community of appropriate scientists. Therefore, it was comparatively easy to rectify errors of judgment.

At present agencies that provide funds do not audit the academic institutions which receive them. Instead, there is an agreement that one government agency will audit a specific institution, without regard for what agency supplies its federal funds. On the whole, academic institutions prefer auditing by the Navy — the Office of Naval Research. The reason for that is that since 1945, the auditors in the Office of Naval

Research have recognized both the character of academia and the purpose of research support, as well as understanding there is little benefit in trying to make the auditing more onerous for the scientist and the university. In contrast, the Department of Health and Human Services is the most vigorous auditor. This is due in part to the fact that the Secretaries of HHS are much more politically aware, or more sensitive to political pressures, than the head of ONR. They set up rules and procedures that may be relevant to the biological sciences, but not necessarily to all the sciences.

The auditors of HHS impose the will of the Secretary, not merely for research supported by HHS, but also by research supported by every other agency in Washington. There is no channel of appeal available to deal with such problems.

It is well to articulate the problem the university faces. Universities have been under a great financial strain, and it is natural for them to increase overhead charges. This is done in good faith. In turn, government auditors have the responsibility to assure us that taxpayers' funds are used properly. Unfortunately, the agreements reached by the administrators in government and in academia never take into account whether the agreement helps the scientific effort, or even whether it provides increased stability for the academic institution. Presidents in a number of universities pay limited interest to this issue, and thus the importance of research to the educational process is not given enough weight.

The selection of individuals to be supported in science presents a problem in a democracy. The recognition of leaders in the sciences isa complex process, involving judgments as to what the important problems are, and who has the ability and talent to best elucidate new experimental or theoretical concepts. A consensus very often takes time to form. There are many examples of delayed recognition, and such recognition most of the time, historically, is made by the leaders in the field. Scientific recognition is not a democratic procedure.

The other side of the coin is that leaders alone, operating at the cutting edge of knowledge, cannot survive without the contributions of a large body of scientists who do distinguished but not very creative work. Careful work, both experimental and theoretical, is necessary for discovering phenomena which demonstrate the consistency or lack of consistency in existing ideas, laws or interpretations. Historically, many young men and women, not yet recognized, have produced revolutionary concepts and experimental results. Thus, the procedure for support should have a democratic aspect, and yet not neglect uniqueness.

With the creation of Brookhaven National Laboratory, a pattern was established that has been used for about 35 years in particle physics and terrestrial astronomy. It has worked very well. Experiments have been selected by scientific groups — often international in character. Theoreticians play an important role and there is informal international competition for time on costly equipment. Americans use facilities in Germany and in Geneva; Russians and Europeans use ours, and budgets are determined annually. Sometimes these budgets are inadequate, but it is important that there are stable institutions and assured continuity.

The administrative structure reports to the Director. Scientific output determines success.

Through the years a procedure has evolved in the authorization and construction of such major experimental facilities. This normally involves the articulation of need by a scientific community, the agreement to such need by the interested executive agency or agencies, and the final approval and appropriation of Congress. Congress has never denied such requests, although at times there have been delays.

The most successful, or productive, laboratories are those that are dedicated to a single area of science. Usually that area is defined by costly equipment or a unique instrument. Generally, those laboratories that are given multiple functions do less distinguished work. The funding agency is continually defining its needs; it continues to intervene in the laboratory's operations, both administratively and in terms of content.

Recently, large university laboratories have been experiencing uncertainties. As a rule, block grants have been decreasing in size, and many have become less stabile. Peer review is responsible for the erosion. Peers contend that these large institutions are privileged and should compete with other potential recipients. The real question is, is the work and output of these labs more distinguished than that of the average peer-review recipient? The answer, at least in limited sampling, is that the output of large laboratories is superior. These labs are needed for scientific accomplishment.

As I said before, progress in experimental science is heavily dependent on instruments. Instruments extend human ability to observe new regions in nature, regions that could not be reached with prior sensing devices, at least not with the necessary precision. In addition, new instruments increase productivity in both experimental and theoretical research. Computers are an excellent example because they effect both experimental and theoretical investigation.

This country needs a long-range plan for scientific instrumentation. Some instruments may cost $5,000 or $10,000. Others may range from a hundred thousand to a million dollars. Very little overhead is involved in the university or government making such acquisitions. Now and then the National Science Foundation receives appropriations of a few million dollars for instruments; however, the nation needs a continuing financial commitment for instruments.

The grant procedure does help, but very often the granting officer or peer-review group reduces the budget by eliminating new instruments. Each new administration and Congress modify tax laws by permitting more rapid write-off on new machinery for industrial purposes to increase productivity and reduce the cost of a final product. Although there are comparable benefits in science, there is no comparable mechanism for the support of academic research. Right now, American research faces foreign competition. There should be a continuing fund appropriated annually for instruments. The National Science Foundation could administer these funds, or they could be distributed among all agencies supporting research.

Our Country has certain unique institutions which several years ago were given block grants to assure their stability. They received funds from a number of agencies, demonstrating that they were performing a unique function. The agencies could designate members of the visiting committee to meet with institution directors, review past results, and plan future undertakings.

Currently, judgment concerning the support of individual scientists involves both the judgment of the agency's granting officer and peer review. This method consumes the most manpower both in government and the university. It is probably the most democratic method as well, but the nature of science is not democratic. The peer-review system now involves thousands of reviewers. This number indicates that it is possible that leaders in science have a limited involvement, and that to serve as a reviewer may be merely honorific. Analysis of the peer-review system demonstrates that the best projects are supported and that, on the average, good science is performed in this country. The general scientific community backs peer review; however, as the number of those engaged in peer review increases, responsibility for specific selections becomes practically nonexistent.

Usually the individual scientist already has a large administrative load. In one institution he or she will be given a book of instruction that is 50 pages long. There are also administrative personnel in universities whose job is to obtain grants or contracts. One finds that on an average, a scientist annually submits or writes three proposals, each at least 25 pages long. There is certain logic to the number three; on the average only one in three is accepted. Compared to other types of support, the individual researcher has the largest administrative burden.

Not all agencies use peer review and perhaps peer review should not be expanded. There are indications that block grants give great freedom to the institution and that the projects selected, whether at a university or other type of scientific institution, tend to have greater scientific validity.

One more note. At times Congress passes legislation that decreases stability in academia and increases administrative burdens both in the government and in academic institutions. While Congress is motivated by the desire to understand what is going on, to determine whether a national purpose is served, and to discover whether their constituency is properly served a price is paid in some of that legislation. It can reduce the productivity of the scientific community, and thus the effectiveness of American science.

The purpose of this paper has been to examine whether or not the administrative overhead in government and universities can be reduced. This issue requires careful thinking by both universities and government agencies because, given the present climate, it will be difficult to convince the public that very little of the large billions of dollars allocated for research are deflected for personal privilege.

A major question is whether more and more decision-making responsibility can be placed in academic institutions, thereby reducing the great structure that has evolved with the peer-review mechanism. Perhaps leaving these decisions to the universities will provide greater opportunities for young and promising scientists who have yet to make visible reputations.

There is a need for greater freedom for scientists to do their work. There is also a need for less monitoring by the government, for less monitoring by the non-academic staffs of universities, and for greater involvement of the presidents of our universities. The result will be increased creativity in our basic scientific effort.

Accountability in Federally-Supported University Research

Linda S. Wilson

Introduction

Habitually, many functions of the federal government have been contracted out to organizations outside the government. This is beneficial because the requisite staff and the flexibility of operations and the work atmosphere can be more readily obtained via the administrative contract, including grants. This is more efficient than creating new, independent agencies or adding to already established Executive departments. In addition, the federal government also awards contracts and grants for other reasons, such as strengthening organizations deemed important to the public interest, stimulating innovation in policy and administration, expanding participation in policy formation, or avoiding centralized bureaucracy. Whether the government's work is done within the government itself or through delegation to outside organizations, federal agencies are answerable to the public for what work is done and for how well it is done. This delegation of responsibility to outside organizations complicates government's accountability to the public; this is especially true when the government contracts for creative endeavors. To produce the maximum incentive both for distinctive and creative contributions, the performing organization needs considerable independence.

The relationships among the outside contractors and grantees, the Executive agencies, Congress, and the public yields a system of checks and balances. The public's principal concern is that public funds be spent wisely, ethically, and fairly, and that waste is minimized and fraud precluded. Since Congress is answerable in a very direct way (election) to the public, its members have a special interest in the performance of government agencies and in preventing both wrong-doing and the appearance of wrong-doing. Executive agencies depend on nongovernment organizations for certain government functions, and the performing organizations depend upon the government for some of their operating budget. In addressing today's concerns about accountability,

Linda S. Wilson is Associate Vice Chancellor for Research and Associate Dean of the Graduate College at the University of Illinois, Urbana-Champaign. She was a member of the National Commission on Research.

it is important not to lose sight of the overall system of these interrelationships.

The last 15 years have brought an increasing emphasis on the accountability and management of public funds. There has been an escalation in the number of institutions participating in grants and contracts with the federal government, in the number of personnel involved in this work, in the number of sponsoring agencies, and in the number of different federal programs involved. Federal funds spent for these purposes have multiplied manifold.

During this same period, the space program fostered expectations about the benefits of applying contemporary management techniques; however, the problems being addressed in various other sectors are harder to approach and more expensive to solve. Persistent economic difficulty has burdened individuals and institutions and confidence in large organizations, government or private, has declined for a number of reasons, including Watergate. Any news of irregularity, fraud, or ethical wrong-doing has become alarming in view of the tremendous growth of federal expenditures and so the public has become increasingly concerned about accountability.

One response to these pressures is to increase controls over federally-supported work, to enforce existing rules more conscientiously, and to introduce additional rules where necessary. Such a response, however, may not always be the most effective means for improving the situation. Indeed, it can exacerbate the problem. Both universities and the government are able to accommodate processes of incremental change much more easily than they accommodate major changes in approach, yet new and different approaches to problems may yield better results. Therefore they, too, need consideration. The challenge here lies in selecting appropriately from an array of approaches.

The stresses mentioned above, the changes in magnitude of the enterprise, the changes in expectations, the economic pressures, etc., have affected other organizations as well as universities. The effect has been to create new demands for accountability from all of these organizations. The problems are neither simple nor unimportant. The issue for all organizations is not whether proper accountability should be provided, but how that accountability can be rendered so that it is simultaneously effective and non-intrusive.

The focus of accountability here will be on a subset of universities, the research universities. The commitment of these universities to research and the magnitude of their involvement with the federal government for research support distinguish them from other colleges and universities. These factors shape not only the problems but also the institution's ability to cope with requirements for accountability.

The Government-University Relationship

Although research universities and the government share some important characteristics, there are deeply rooted institutional differences between them. In addition, their relationship is complicated by the very characteristics which they hold in common. They are both highly complex, evolving, and diverse institutions; they both have limited resources and must wrestle with their own conflicting goals. Their relationship is particularly vulnerable to strain for two reasons. First, the relationship is a composite relationship. It is made up of many individual relationships, and few participants perceive the whole picture. Second, both the nature and operating methods of the two partners are quite different. This can lead to a serious mismatch of expectations. Furthermore, both the government and the universities have leaders who hold a variety of views on the proper relationship between the government and the universities.

During the past ten years, concern about accountability in the university-government research relationship has escalated. The 1979 report of the Department of Health, Education and Welfare (HEW), Office of the Inspector General [1] stated that HEW auditors had set 5.7 percent of the total university expenditures aside as unauditable because the universities' systems of accounting did not allow them to determine whether those expenditures had been properly charged. While setting aside expenditures does not indicate the charges were illegal or improper, it does mean that they could not be audited under existing regulations and thus must be adjudicated. It also indicates that there is a serious lack of agreement about proper documentation standards. HEW auditors also reported that 0.23 percent of the total expenditures reviewed were not properly charged. While an auditor's report is a finding, such findings are not necessarily sustained through the subsequent steps of institutional response and resolution. It seems clear, however, that there are important differences between government financial management personnel and the universities as to what constitutes evidence of proper stewardship for federal funds.

In its 1980 report on accountability,[2] the National Commission on Research reviewed the major areas of concern about accountability in the government-university relationship. That report cited the government auditors' dissatisfaction with the documentation practices of universities, particularly their systems of documenting charges to salaries and wages, cost sharing, consultants, and cost transfers. The auditors also found deficiencies in certain university management systems. The Commission report also reviewed the universities' concerns, including what they perceive to be an increasing emphasis on fiscal and administrative accountability without due regard for the scientific accountability provided in peer reviews, program reviews, and technical reports. The universities point both to an escalation in the standards of documentation imposed by the auditors, which fuel outside the regular processes for negotiation, and to the promulgation of new standards. The universities are concerned about what they consider an over-emphasis on accounting precision and uniformity, and they are concerned about unrealistic expectations about the validity of certain accountability procedures such as effort reporting. They object to the continuing lack of reimbursement for certain kinds of research costs. In addition, they raise serious questions about the validity and fairness of certain auditing practices and they express doubt about the integrity of the audit resolution process as it has been operating. The Commission summarized these disagreements:

1. the university accounting systems are inadequate for stewardship of public funds; and
2. the government procedures do not appropriately allow for the conditions required to discover new knowledge or for the multi-product nature of the activities in research universities.

There is evidence in both informal reports of scientists and administrators and informal government reports that problems of accountability have been increasing. When universities began expressing increasing concern about significant changes in their audit relationships, despite the absence of any formal changes in policy or procedures, one of the university associations initiated an Audit Information Exchange.[3] This allowed institutions to share their audit reports confidentially. The Exchange distributed a newsletter which gave digests of the audit reports and identified both the questions raised by auditors and the institutions' responses. The principal audit questions concerned inadequacies in salary and wage documentation, late or undocumented costs transfers, and undocumented consultant costs.

The University of Miami prepared a case study[4] of its experience with HEW audits which demonstrated that the audit report is not the final step and may not provide an accurate picture of the adequacy of an institution's system of accountability.

One report from the General Accounting Office,[5] based on an examination of records at six institutions, concluded that serious deficiencies exist in university accounting systems. It urged "tightening up" the cost principles to improve accountability. A second GAO report[6] criticized both HEW for its auditing performance and the universities for their accounting systems. The report expressed concern that Federal audits are falling short of the quality contemplated by the GAO *Standard for Audit of Governmental Organizations, Programs, Activities, and Functions.*[7]

Evidence of the deteriorating government-university research relationship is largely descriptive and anecdotal. The difficulty of documenting in any quantitative way the costs of increased regulation and the lost opportunities, the dimunition of motivation and the losses in morale, discourages attempts at analytical studies. Nevertheless, Smith and Karlesky, in their book *The State of Academic Science,*[8] describe deep concern about "the subtle extension of inflexible controls that limit individual researcher's freedom of action" which they learned about in their site visits to six departments in each of 36 institutions. Informal surveys of faculty[9][10] identified concern about the detrimental effects of the proliferation of federally-mandated inefficient bureaucracy on campus, erected in the name of accountability.

In 1977, the Sloan Commission on Government and Higher Education[11] invited 21 colleges and universities to examine the impact of the federal government on them, each in its own way. They were asked to consider their relationships with the government, both as regulator and as patron in the provision of student aid and research support. In the research area, the institutions' responses focused particularly on the burden of effort reporting and on its incompatability with both educational institutions and the research process, on reporting requirements, on fiscal regulations enforcement methods, and, finally, on regulations for human subjects.

One unfortunate result of the allegations and counter-allegations has been a loss of confidence in the universities, in the government, and, to a lesser extent, in the research they undertake together. Some of the participants have lost confidence in their counterparts in the relationship. It is significant, and reassuring, that this loss of confidence is concentrated in the administrative and financial areas and has not yet spread to scientific personnel.

It is essential that the government and the universities, individually and jointly, carefully examine the nature of their disagreements and the deteriorating effect the conflict has on their relationship. They must also construct remedies for the problems. The national interest is not served by diminished confidence either in universities, research or the government: the nation cannot afford a situation in which the government's stewardship for federal funds is undermined; the nation cannot afford to damage universities as institutions by inappropriate and intrusive requirements; the nation is not served if the environment in which research is performed becomes stifling instead of stimulating and supportive. The relationship between the government and the universities involves an interdependence developed over the years as the two have cooperated in pursuit of knowledge for the public welfare. This relationship has been extraordinarily fruitful in scientific achievement. The quality of that relationship must be restored.

Speculation about the reasons for the allegations and counter-allegations which reflect the problems and contribute to the deterioration of the relationship yields a number of possibilities. Perhaps the universities have become opportunistic, or worse, dishonest, and perhaps they are in fact diverting federal research funds for unintended purposes. On the other hand, perhaps the expectations of government and the university differ. Perhaps the agreements between them have been somewhat ambiguous. Alternatively, the methods for testing accountability may be wrong or inappropriate for the nature of the institutions and processes involved. Or perhaps the government needs a scapegoat. The government's problems are many and complex — some say intractable. Maybe the government's struggle with the universities is simply a conscious or unconscious way of deflecting attention from other problems and of demonstrating its commitment to accountability. Or, perhaps the government really is attempting to exploit the universities, to pass on more of the burden of support of research to the institutions. Alternatively the reasons could be that resources are scarce and the allocation of them among competing needs and demands is excrutiatingly difficult. Such pressures can quite naturally lead to attempts to centralize and increase controls over expenditures. One further possibility is that priorities are being re-ordered and that some participants in the relationship are either unaware of the re-ordering or are in disagreement with it.

Some of the reasons suggested above can be ruled out as insignificant, if they contribute at all. Although occasional abuse can occur in universities, as in other organizations, there simply is no evidence to support significant evidence of a pattern of intentional scapegoating or exploitation of universities by the government. The other reasons suggested above are far more plausible.

The report on accountability issued by the National Commission on Research[12] attributes the problem to several causes. These include certain historical developments, such as changes in the character in the relationship, changes in the nature of federal support for research, changes in the institutions themselves, and changes in the research climate. In addition to these historical developments, the Commission identified the fundamental process and organizational differences between the government and the universities, the basic design of the research support system, and some operational problems as sources of strain.

Creative adjustment of the relationship is complicated by the nature of the organizations involved and their roles in our society. While the partnership is designed to take advantage of areas of mutual interest and objectives, it must accommodate the tension of conflicting goals essential to the function of each of the partners.

Since the question is not the need for accountability for public funds used in support of research, but the terms on which such accountability should be secured, it is important to identify the policy issues which must be addressed in resolving this question.

Policy Issues

There are four major policy issues central to the discussion of how accountability should be rendered in the government-university research relationship. Debate and resolution of these issues would improve the relationship.

The first of these policy issues is the set of factors which must be considered in developing principles or procedures for accountability in the government-university relationship. Some of the present problems of accountability may well be the result of overlooking or disregarding some of the important factors involved.

Fundamental Principles of the Partners

One of the factors to be considered is the set of fundamental principles which defines the purposes and guides the actions of the partners involved. For example, the pursuit of knowledge is a principal function of research universities. Freedom of inquiry, institutional diversity and the interweaving of research and teaching are critical elements in the performance of that function. The fundamental principles for the government are that public funds must be spent in the public interest, that public support demands public accountability, and that the nation's system of checks and balances and the distribution of responsibility imposes certain constraints. Acceptable principles of accountability will be those which are compatible with the principles of both partners.

Nature and Purposes of Relationship

A second factor is the nature and purposes of the relationship between the partners. The relationship exists on two levels. There is a kind of overall relationship between the set of universities and the government in all of its parts. Together the government and the universities are able to do what neither could do as well alone. This is a very broad relationship, one for which it is difficult to define boundaries. It has a philosophical basis. In this country, freedom of thought and speech are highly valued. We have formally separated our institutions of higher education from the government as one way of preserving those freedoms. We have developed basic science primarily in the universities in order to avoid central control of science or the establishment of orthodoxies. Nevertheless, the government has a high stake in the quality of the education and the strength of the research enterprise. Therefore, the government stimulates research and education in areas of public concern, invests in innovation, studies the processes involved, but stops short of intruding in the curriculum or supporting the basic operating costs of the institutions.

In some countries the government finances both the instructional and research functions of the universities directly, so that the question of distinguishing the university's and government's objectives in these areas does not arise. In the United States, government and universities have differing goals, but some overlapping objectives. However, it is essential that both partners recognize that the mutuality of goals and objectives is not complete. This is an essential ingredient in accountability, but often the purpose of the relationship is not clearly articulated, perhaps it is intentionally allowed to remain vague. Sometimes the purpose is simply assumed or implied, as though it were obvious. Furthermore, there can be confusion between "what is" and "what ought to be"; wishful thinking occurs on both sides of the relationship. In addition, understandings and opinions about the purpose of the relationship evolve gradually and not always congruently.

In addition to the overall relationship, there are also the specific relationships which involve a single university with a federal agency, program by program, project by project, or investigator by investigator. In these relationships, too, there are some common objectives, some overlapping of goals. But there are boundaries too. Some of the participants in these specific relationships do not always realize that the agreement is not unlimited.

One way to look at this problem is to recognize that there are several continua involved. There is the continuum of possible arrangements, ranging from highly constrained agreements,to agreements in principle with details to be worked out later. There is the continuum of support, ranging from broad support for a general purpose to narrow support for specific categories of activity. Often there is confusion in applying procedures of accountability appropriate for categorical support in situations where the support was intended to general support. There is also a kind of continuum in terms of the government's purpose. Sometimes the government "buys" to suit a federal need or for federal use.

Sometimes the government's acquisition or support is aimed at a specific federal mission. There are other situations in which a federal purpose is involved, but the performers and beneficiaries are not the government itself. The final continuum is that of control and responsibility.

It is intellectually appealing to create some sort of scheme to label and develop scales for these characteristics. Then the interactions among the various continua could be modeled and perhaps optimal templates for management and accountability could be designed. Characteristics of specific projects could be fed into an algorithm, yielding a prescription for appropriate management and requirements for accountability. Such a mechanistic approach should not replace the judgment of knowledgeable decision-makers; however it is important to recognize these continua and to address the full range of opportunities for judgment they present.

Nature of Activity

Another factor is the nature of the activity to be undertaken. Creative activities make different demands on the relationship and the procedures for accountability than do production, manufacturing, or service activities. The latter are more easily planned. Their beginning and ending points are more easily defined, and it is relatively straightforward to evaluate the effectiveness of the steps in between. Such activities traverse known territory. Conversely, in a creative enterprise, discovery is the objective. Constraints on freedom must be limited to stimulate creativity and to allow for serendipity. New ideas and new approaches, i.e., changes, are the rule, not the exception. Such activities are much more difficult to circumscribe or to forecast. The evaluation of effectiveness focuses primarily on the outcome, not the process. The closeness with which the outcome reflects the original objectives of the work may not be an appropriate criterion by which the outcome is judged.

Currently, recognition of the difference between research and manufacturing or production is not sufficient. In addition, significant variations in the nature of various research activities must be better understood. These differences must be taken into account in the design of management procedures, including those for accountability, because some procedures which are effective for applied research, development, testing, or documentation would be intrusive, inhibiting, and counterproductive for basic research.

The Nature of the Organization

The nature of the organization in which the activity will take place must also be considered in the design of accountability procedures. It is axiomatic to fit the processes of management to the nature of the organization in which they will have to operate. What is sometimes missing, however, is a genuine understanding of what features are essential to the nature of the organization. This is particularly likely to happen when the essential features are different for the different organizations in the relationship. The nature of an organization depends on its charter, its missions or functions, its history, and its traditions. It also depends on its governance, particularly on who makes the decisions and by what processes those decisions are made. Government and universities are quite different in this respect, and for good reason. The reasons for and implications of the decentralized, self-ruling character of universities is not widely understood outside these organizations. Similarly, the complexity of government decision-making, imposed by the system of checks and balances and the breadth of government's constituencies, is not always understood by those outside government. Other elements which shape the nature of the organization are the sources of its funds, the limits on its resources, and the entities to which it is accountable for its performance. All these elements influence the development of the organization's operating principles and its criteria for decisions. They shape the constraints on the organization's flexibility in accepting externally imposed requirements and in accommodating change in general.

Specific Objectives for Accountability

The design of procedures and policies must be informed by the attributes to be fostered, the problems to be solved, and the dangers to be avoided. These must be examined realistically to determine whether the best approach is to impose control, to set rules or suggest guidelines, or to employ incentives.

Cost-Benefit Ratio

Finally, the relative costs and benefits of alternative approaches must be considered. The processes of accountability themselves must meet the tests of accountability. In weighing the costs and benefits, it is important to identify all of them, including such elements as the costs of lost research time and the benefits of the preventive role which procedures of accountability can play. Questions of independence of review, reliability of data, and materiality of breaches in the requirements are significant. In this, as in other areas, the nature of the risks must be examined along with their consequences, the probability of their occurring, and the difficulty of developing strategies to contain them. A risk-free system is probably impossible, even if it could be afforded. In any population there will be some entrepreneurs, opportunists, and cheaters. Neither the universities nor the government are immune. To a certain extent, however, the rules themselves define, somewhat arbitrarily, who fits in these categories. For rules and laws to be effective, they must fit the situation, have some logical basis, and reflect the mores of the majority of those whom they govern. Laws and rules which lack such a solid basis do not work well; they undermine respect for the government and other institutions.

In addition to the several factors which must be considered in the design of procedures for accountability, there are three other issues. The first of these is the effect the mechanisms used for support of research have on the management and stewardship of public funds awarded for research. There is a life cycle of research agreements which includes three primary stages: the first stage is the selection of research to be supported; the second is the conduct of the research; and the third is the reporting of research results and accounting for resources. Each of these stages involves different facets of accountability and different participants. Unfortunately, the operating understandings and procedures of one stage do not always interact constructively with those of another stage. This is particularly true of the project grant or contract support mechanism, which is the backbone of the system by which federal funds are awarded for research in universities.

Approximately 60 percent of the federal funds expended in universities for research in 1979 were awarded through the mechanism of project grants.[13] These funds are awarded based on proposals submitted by one or a small group of principal investigators who define the research objectives and identify the methodology they plan to use in reaching these objectives. Such proposals are commonly evaluated through a peer-review system. Each award is a separate agreement between the sponsor and the performing institution; each requires individual review, as well as individual accounting and reporting. A single major research university is likely to have one to two hundred such agreements operating at the same time, all with different principal investigators, different objectives, and different contractual periods.

The project system emphasizes the selection stage. The detailed research proposals, which are useful in choosing among a large number of projects, and also serve as a straightjacket for research if latitude for the opportunities and exigencies of research is not present in the performance and reporting stages. The segregation of research into specific projects enhances the selection stage, but complicates the post-award administration of research. It emphasizes compartmentalization, at the expense of interrelating lines of inquiry and facilitating the effectiveness of research management. The project system gives flexibility to the sponsoring agencies in changing direction or priorities, but it can interfere with the development of coherent research programs by individual investigators and research organizations, if the compartmentalization is rigorously imposed in the performance and reporting stages.

Even though the project system involves agreements between the sponsoring government agency and the university, the principal relationship is between the agency and the individual faculty member. In the university environment, this strengthens the autonomy of the individual faculty member. While this is consistent with the design of the university itself, such autonomy does not always lend itself to the management processes developed for more hierarchical organizational structures. It complicates the imposition of administrative regimentation. Finally, the expectations of and understandings between the agency and university scientific personnel who participate in these stages are not always understood or accepted by administrative and financial personnel. All participants need to develop a better understanding about what is legitimate and need to recognize that favoring isolated parts of the overall system has an impact, which is not necessarily beneficial, on all other parts of the system.

The next policy issue to be considered is the availability of effective management technology for the research relationship between government and universities. Much of the present technology for the management of large and complex institutions has been developed through studies of business and industry or of government organizations. Procedures and priorities which are appropriate in these organizations are not necessarily transferable to non-profit research organizations, especially universities. Furthermore, many of the tools for accountability presently applied in the government-university relationship are adapted from those derived for the process of government procurement of materials and services.

The research relationship does not fit comfortably in the procurement mold. The accounting principles for cost reimbursement in a procurement often seem to constrain the relationship rather than support it. The present problems of accountability in the research relationship arise, in large part, because of fundamental inadequacies of the model in use. In earlier years, allowances were made by both partners for the crudeness of the model; today's demands call for closer tolerances. A prime example is the requirement for documentation of salaries and wages charged to federally-sponsored research projects. The cost reimbursement mode places the government's objective of stewardship in conflict with the joint-product character of academic work and the intentional avoidance of standardized work loads for faculty in research universities.

The third major policy issue which must be addressed in order to resolve the current problems of accountability is which priorities should be followed where compromises or trade-offs are required. This issue is a corollary to the first policy issue mentioned. In so complex a system, it is impossible to find solutions for problems which do not require some balance among competing needs. This is true at both the macro- and micro-level. That is, the issue is relevant for the government-university relationship in its broadest terms, and it also present in the minute decisions made by the investigator during the life of a particular project. Conflicts arise between what will yield the best research results and what will provide the closest adherence to financial or administrative requirements.

Overall accountability includes both scientific accountability and financial and administrative accountability. The objectives of these two differ. Scientific accountability focuses on achievement of results or progress toward proposed scientific objectives. The focus of financial and administrative accountability is on financial propriety and compliance with administrative requirements. A well-designed system of accountability involves an appropriate balance of these objectives. In arriving at that balance, priorities must first be determined, and the determination of those priorities requires an agreement about the criteria to be used.

Illustrative Problems in Accountability

Universities have been severely criticized for inadequate accounting systems. Two problem areas — effort reporting systems and cost transfers — illustrate the need to address the policy issues described above.

Effort Reporting

The struggle over effort reporting is not new. More than once in the history of the relationship between government and universities, representatives from both sides have attempted to derive a resolution to the problem. Several different methods have been put forward but neither party subsequently found the compromise satisfactory.[14]

The government has sought assurance that federal funds are used for their intended purposes. Given that federal support of research in universities results from an overlap of interests between itself and the universities, the government seeks to reimburse its fair share of the costs while avoiding the unintentional support of other institutional functions. The government's standard has been the industrial model, which employs frequent reporting on an after-the-fact basis in terms of time or effort expended. Such reporting, however, is foreign to the academic environment, in which faculty operate on the basis of work assignments.

Because the activity of professional personnel in universities has a complex, multi-purpose, joint-product character, the universities judge accountability through performance. Time and effort are considerations in assigning workload for professional personnel in universities, but neither hours worked nor effort expended is used as a measure of performance. Evaluation of performance is based on outcome: the quality of work produced, its significance, the competency of students taught, client satisfaction, etc. In research universities, the quality and quantity of the outcome of research, as assessed by peers, is a major factor in recruitment, promotion, granting of tenure, and continuing performance evaluation of faculty and other professionals.

Universities carry out their research, service, and instruction as an integrated whole, not as separate and isolated functions. Most faculty work serves several purposes. Allocation of activity among several functions is necessarily an arbitrary assignment. Government and universities differ markedly in the value placed on such information.

The recent struggle to revise the federal cost principles for colleges and universities sprang from the desire of government and universities to find more satisfactory methods for accountability. Unfortunately, the revised cost principles are not sufficient either.

Much of the continuing difficulty regarding appropriate accountability for salaries and wages charged to federally-sponsored agreements can be explained as the result of inadequate attention to some of the factors which are critical in the design of management procedures. For example, the present procedures make inadequate provision for certain fundamental characteristics of one of the participating organizations (integration of teaching, research and services in universities). They either do not fully support the nature and purposes of the government-university relationship, or they demonstrate a fundamental difference of expectations for that relationship, at least for some of the participants. They also overlook certain operating principles of the institutions (evaluation based upon performance, not effort or time expended).

Improved management techniques for accountability could both meet government's legitimate need for assurance of proper stewardship and yet make sense for universities.

Cost Transfers

The term "cost transfers" refers to retroactive transfers of charges from one account to another. Auditors review them carefully to see whether they reflect proper or improper use of restricted funds. For the last several years, audit reports have repeatedly cited instances of unreasonably late, improper, and inadequately documented cost transfers.

In part, these cost transfer problems arise from the conflicting expectations of the auditors and the scientific officers of the agency. The officers focus on the scientific reason for a transfer and the interrelationship of projects, while the auditors seek a clear segregation of costs for separately funded projects. Such differences represent varying interpretations of the principle of allocability stated in OMB Circular A-21.

The cost transfer problem is also due to the design of the system, in which support for research comes in multiple, discrete, project awards of limited duration. Where an individual investigator's overall research program is funded via several different research agreements, some costs may be assigned as legitimately to one source as to another. Furthermore, effective management of the resources may require retroactive reallocation of charges.

An unfortunate but commonplace occurrence, the delayed arrival of award notices, generates additional cost transfers. Often institutions must draw upon their own funds to initiate purchase orders and continue personnel support and thereby avoid serious gaps or delays. Subsequently, these charges must be transferred to the correct account once the award is received.

Where the cost transfer reflects an unauthorized diversion of funds for purposes unrelated to the scope of the support agreement, the transfer is clearly improper and unallowable. The difficulty lies in distinguishing legitimate transfers from illegitimate ones without overburdening the system with requirements for documentation or inflexibility.

In 1980, the National Commission on Research formulated a set of recommendations based on its analysis of the accountability problems.[15] These recommendations addressed the three basic areas: *1.* improvement of the relationship through better understanding of the nature, driving forces, and constraints of the partners; *2.* specific adjustments of the accountability requirements which are causing difficulty; and *3.* development of a more flexible and facilitating environment for research. The Commission's recommendations were as follows:

1. The Commission recommends that research universities and the government make vigorous, concerted efforts to overcome the mutual suspicions, ignorance, and misunderstandings which strain their relationship and weaken the nation's research enterprise.

2. The Commission recommends that research universities and the government develop a new system for accountability tailored to the nature of the activity being sponsored and based on a set of minimum core requirements applicable to all research agreements. The core requirements would be sufficient for all basic research and some applied research; further requirements would be added only for activities of a pronounced procurement character.

3. The Commission recommends that the Office of Management and Budget, in consultation with the federal agencies which sponsor research and the universities, revise the federal cost principles (Circular A-21) and the federal management principles (Circular A-110) as soon as possible, but certainly within three to five years. The revision should assure that these guidelines for financial and adminnstrative accountability: (1) incorporate features which not only control against abuse but also facilitate and encourage effective management, (2) are fully consistent with the nature of the research process, (3) accommodate better to the academic environment in which they must operate, and (4) are based on better mutual understanding of the purposes of the government-university research relationship.

4. The Commission recommends, as a minimum, that the Office of Management and Budget institute new procedures to allow an opportunity for research funding agencies to comment on draft audit findings covering their university projects. This arrangement would be roughly parallel with current practices involving draft GAO management audit reports, and would provide relevant information for the audit agency.

5. In addition to the above review, the Commission recommends, as an optimum, that agency program officers supplement their review of final scientific reports with advisory observations concerning reasonableness, from a research standpoint, of the expenditures for personnel. The records of sponsoring agencies subsequently would be useful for the independent financial audits. This would link the technical review and the financial audit, an important linkage now missing.

6. The Commission recommends a simpler and less costly method of effort reporting based on responsible self-regulation: the explicit certification by individual investigators that direct salary charges to their research agreements are reasonable and fair, coupled with the federal program officer's review of the reasonableness of these expenditures for the work undertaken.

7. The Commission recommends that government agencies and universities jointly construct an option, analogous to the "standard deduction" in income tax calculation, to charge activity which is treated as indirect costs under sponsored agreements. The fixed percentage would be negotiated. It might either be uniform or vary from institution to institution. Some universities would not receive full credit for their allowable indirect costs. However, accountability would be fully served and both government and universities would reduce the burden of detailed accounting and audit.

8. The Commission recommends that university presidents review their financial management systems. Universities should invest sufficient resources to ensure adequate control and accounting for the expenditure of research funds. These systems must provide timely and accurate financial information necessary for effective research management by research investigators. In turn, research investigators must meet the responsibilities and obligations which accompany their use of public funds.

9. The Commission recommends that the government and universities develop revised financial and scientific accountability processes which increase the flexibility and incentives for investigators to manage research funds in a scientifically prudent manner.

10. The Commission recommends that agencies delegate to the universities more authority to make budgeting and management decisions under sponsored agreements.

11. The Commission recommends that Congress authorize and agencies develop arrangements for aggregating individual research projects for administrative purposes.

12. The Commission recommends that government agencies improve the management of research funds by eliminating unnecessary constraints on the timing of expenditures. Specifically, the Commission recommends institutional authorization for pre-award expenditures up to 90 days prior to the effective date of awards and for carryover of surpluses or deficits to the following contractual period, at least up to a specified percentage of the total award for that period. This involves no risk or commitment by the sponsoring agency.

13. The Commission recommends that Congress, the agencies, and the universities assure that the processes of accountability themselves meet the tests of accountability. The processes should yield results which justify their cost. One important application of this principle would be the elimination of the documentation now required by legislated cost-sharing on research grants.

The purpose of the National Commission on Research was to review the key elements of the present state of federally supported university research, to analyze problem areas, and to provide suggestions for actions to alleviate these problems. Given the diversity of federal agencies, universities, investigators, and fields of activity that are involved, the Commission recognized that consensus on all issues would be elusive.

Conclusion

The purpose of this paper has been to expand the discussion of one aspect of the government-university relationship, namely accountability, and to draw attention to the basic policy issues which must be addressed in the design of constructive accountability policies and procedures. The nature of the accountability problems which currently afflict the relationship suggests that all participants in the government-university relationship need to give serious thought to these policy issues. Furthermore, it would seem advisable for the graduate training of future participants in this relationship to include presentation of information on the nature and fundamental principles of the partner organizations, some historical perspectives on their relationship, and exposure to the kinds of policy issues which arise. Genuine mutual understanding should foster development of constructive solutions to today's problems.

REFERENCES

1. Office of Inspector General, D.H.E.W., *Annual Report,* January 1, 1978 — December 31, 1978 (U.S. Government Printing Office, Washington, D.C., 1979).

2. National Commission on Research, *Accountability: Restoring the Quality of the Partnership* (Washington, D.C.: National Commission on Research, March 1980), p. 7.

3. Committee on Governmental Relations, *Audit Information Exchange Newsletter,* (Committee on Governmental Relations, Washington, D.C.).

4. John L. Green, Jr., "A Case Study of D.H.E.W. Audit of Direct and Indirect Costs," presented at the Tenth Annual Professional Development Workshop, Central Association of Colleges and University Business Officers, St. Louis, Mo., February 1978.

5. General Accounting Office, *Federally Sponsored Research at Educational Institutions: A Need for Improved Accountability,* (U.S. Government Printing Office, Washington, D.C., 1978).

6. General Accounting Office, *Need for More Effective Audits of Federal Grants and Contracts Administered by Institutions of Higher Education* (U.S. Government Printing Office, Washington, D.C., 1979).

7. General Accounting Office, *Standards for Audit of Governmental Organizations, Programs, Activities, and Functions,* (Government Printing Office, Washington, D.C., 1974).

8. Bruce L.R. Smith and Joseph J. Karlesky, *The State of Academic Science: The Universities in the Nation's Research Efforts,* Vol. I, *Summary of Major Findings,* (New Rochelle, N.Y.: Change Magazine Press, 1977).

9. Philip H. Abelson, "Problems of Science Faculties," *Science,* April 13, 1979, p. 133.

10. National Science Foundation Advisory Council. "Accountability in Research: Report of Task Group #7," October, 1979.

11. Irene K. Spero, *Government and Higher Education, A Summary of Twenty-One Institutional Self Studies,* Sloan Commission on Government and Higher Education, 1978.

12. National Commission on Research, *Accountability: Restoring the Quality of the Partnership* (Washington, D.C.: National Commission on Research, March 1980), p. 9.

13. National Commission on Research, *Funding Mechanisms: Balancing Objectives and Resources in University Research* (Washington, D.C.: National Commission on Research, May 1980).

14. Neal Hines, *Study of Effort Reporting,* (Committee on Governmental Relations, Washington, D.C., 1975).

15. National Commission on Research, *Accountability: Restoring the Quality of the Partnership* (Washington, D.C.: National Commission on Research, March, 1980), p. 19.

A Bridge Reconnecting Universities and Industry Through Basic Research

Richard E. Lyon, Jr.

The lack of innovation in the United States has become a serious national concern. While obviously a complex problem, one aspect is cited frequently:[1] industry has not benefited from university basic research to the degree necessary for effective innovation, and operative, academic-industrial "connections" need reconstruction in order to correct the situation. This paper suggests an approach to such a reconstruction.

This proposal is not new except perhaps in its detail, but its time may now be here. The proposal is based on the following fundamentals:

- The "connection" should be at the seed of the innovation process — basic research. The paramount goal should be to increase the nation's innovation effectiveness and the process should exploit the individual strengths of our academic and industrial institutions.
- The linkage must be a functioning connection, not simply another point of contact. Many forms of "bridges" have been proposed and careful review suggests they all may help to some extent. But, only direct industry financial support and closer interaction with university basic research capture all the essential features of an operative "connection."
- Government's role should be to support the process of creating the connection. Government should recognize that it is not the primary user of the results and therefore should not attempt to steer the science and technology.
- A significant tax incentive is the appropriate step for establishing "the connection" and helping it to grow to a targeted level. Encouraging wide participation and allowing research to respond to real needs and demands are two of the many advantages of the tax mechanism.
- Industry funding should both supplement and complement federal basic research spending, not totally replace it, since many national objectives would not attract industry attention.

Much has been written on academic-industrial connections and today many companies are working to build these connections. This paper suggests ways to expand these initial efforts and to extend them beyond the large, "well-heeled" organizations that are prepared to risk undertaking such programs within today's tax structure.

Development of such a proposal requires identifying essential elements of a working connection and carefully examining the effec-

---

Richard E. Lyon, Jr. is Vice President for Petroleum Research at Exxon Research and Engineering Company.

tiveness of specific mechanisms to promote the coupling. It is instructive to begin with the current situation.

The Current Situation

Industry's ability to influence and benefit from university basic research has declined dramatically. During the late 1960's and early 1970's, industrial funding of university basic research increased in real terms by about 50 percent (Figure 1). Industry funding in 1972 dollars grew from about $35 million in the early 1960's to about $55 million in 1975. However, since that time, funding has flattened.[2] In parallel, sharp increases in government spending caused a steady drop in the industry

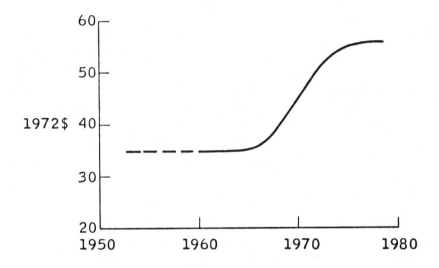

Figure 1. Industrial Funding for
Basic University Research

share of support for university research (Figure 2). During the 1970's, industry only supported a little over two percent of university basic research. The academic-industrial "connection" had been broken!

While the "good old days" were deficient in some respects, universities lost the perspective afforded by the industrial connection, and university basic research became dependent on the government for support and continued health.

The tremendous growth in federal funding has had additional implications. First, many researchers, trained at universities, elected to stay in academia because research funding made it possible. This weakened the "people-link" between industry and academia and made communications more difficult with time. Also, federal dollars were directed to research with limited relevance to industry. Industrial interests are concentrated in the physical and engineering sciences. Today, industry puts about 75 percent of its effort into these areas and

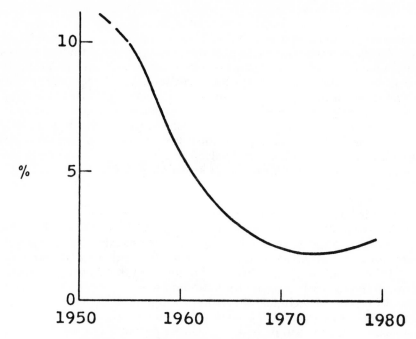

Figure 2. Basic University Research:
Industrial Participation Down

about 15 percent into life sciences. Conversely, physical and engineering science make up only about 30 percent of university basic research, and life sciences constitute about 50 percent.[3]

While all this was taking place, industry research emphasis shifted away from basic research. Since 1966, when spending hit 588 million in 1972 dollars, industrial basic research has consistently declined, to a low of 442 million dollars in 1975. It was hovered around this low and unhealthy level ever since.

In all probability, this is not due to disenchantment with basic research. Rather, basic research has a small present value when viewed in cold economic terms, and it is now generally accepted that benefits cannot always be captured by private firms.[4] Anything short of a new industry, such as xerography or semi-conductors, discounted for 20 or more years at any reasonable value of money, has a small present value. This puts basic research at the economic margin for industry. Expanding federal regulations and uncertainties about the future have caused industry to pull back and move toward shorter term, less risky research — "defensive research." Moreover, these factors are probably more severe in smaller and immature firms which can least afford the expansion required to carry out such defensive research. Overall, without encouragement industry will continue to underinvest in basic research.

Present limits on science funding require that nonproductive claims on research funds be examined constantly. Federal support for basic research has followed the trend of industry basic research. In real terms, shrinking government support changed direction in the past few years, but the revised version of the FY 1981 budget and the Reagan version of the FY 1982 budget suggest that government is not committed to this trend. Overhead and administrative costs associated with federal programs are an added burden. For instance, about six percent of the NSF budget is for program development and management.[5] This is a small fraction of the total budget, but it does consume taxpayer dollars earmarked for research. The hidden costs of securing federal grants and complying with reporting and administrative procedures takes a much larger and ever-expanding cut. Abelson suggests a third or more of the money "ostensibly appropriated for research is being creamed off by university administrators to support federally mandated or inspired bureaucracies."[6]

This brief survey of the current situation suggests numerous deficiencies. In terms of national needs, the most important involve: 1. inefficient dissemination of research results, and 2. focusing basic research away from important industrial problems. Problems of dissemination stem from delays in the publication process and the growing difficulty encountered by the private sector in finding relevant results in the ever-increasing bulk of technical literature. Problems of applicability trace back to the limited nature of private sector guidance and involvement in university basic research, and thus directly contribute to inefficient dissemination of results.

The "Connection" and Innovation

The most obvious reasons to rebuild a functioning academic-industrial connection are because industry can offer useful support when federal budgets are tight, and because industry needs both new and relevant basic science which is both new and relevant to promote its commercial progress. Solow has demonstrated this statistically by showing that more than half the growth in U.S. productivity is due to the advancement of scientific knowledge.[7] Obviously, universities can help fill this vacuum. But the most fundamental reason has to do with the nature of the innovation process itself. It is instructive in this regard to consider our foreign competition.

The following is based on data from Science Indicators — 1978. The data are confounded by many interacting variables and experts are skeptical of their validity, but they are the best we have. Accordingly, conclusions drawn from analysis of this are almost indefensible. However, the data trends are intriguing and support a thesis which is axiomatic (at least for a research manager): effectiveness in moving research to commercialization depends largely on the "quality" and less on the quantity of research actually performed. Alternatively, there are also key ingredients in a successful research program that need careful and constant attention.

A lot has been said about the declining productivity in the United States. Growth of productivity is a measure, in part, of an economy's effectiveness in translating research results into commercial practice.

Recently, the growth of productivity in the United States has been decreasing, giving rise to much concern and discussion. Table 1 shows productivity, roughly over the last two decades, for five major industrial countries. Here, it is defined as "output per worker hour" and is shown as percentage productivity increase normalized to 1960. The concern and consequent public outcry is justified: the United States had the smallest relative growth and of course, Japan had the highest.

Table 2 suggests that the amount of national research and development has little influence on productivity growth. Here total R&D expenditures, as a percent of GNP, show R&D activity relative to the size of the

TABLE 1. PRODUCTIVITY
GROWTH, 1960 — 1977 (percent)

UNITED STATES	60
UNITED KINGDOM	65
FRANCE	150
WEST GERMANY	150
JAPAN	280

TABLE 2. RELATIVE R&D
EXPENDITURES, 1967

	% OF GNP
UNITED STATES	2.9
UNITED KINGDOM	2.3
FRANCE	2.1
WEST GERMANY	2.0
JAPAN	1.5

economy for 1967, which is near the middle of the period considered in Table 1. The numbers change slightly for other years, but the general observation remains the same. Significantly, the ranking of countries by productivity growth over the last 20 years is inverse to the ranking by relative R&D expenditures. The United States spent the most relative to the size of its economy and Japan the least.

However, a different trend appears when one examines who paid for the R&D. The percent of total R&D paid for by business, the potential user, is shown in Table 3 for the same five countries. Again there is a

TABLE 3. BUSINESS SUPPORT OF
R&D, 1967

	% OF TOTAL
UNITED STATES	33
UNITED KINGDOM	43
FRANCE	31
WEST GERMANY	58
JAPAN	62

rough trend, with the United States and Japan at opposite ends. The inference is that the roles of potential users of research results and related matters are at least as important as the amount of research and development actually performed.

Just as a research program requires certain ingredients to be successful, the connection between industry and academia must also contain critical elements to contribute productively to the nation's innova-

tion effectiveness. These elements must be understood before mean-
ingful ways to rebuild the linkage can be proposed and progress
evaluated.

Essential Elements for the Connection

The principal connection between industry and academia should be
in the area of basic research — research geared to searching for new
knowledge and phenomena. Basic research is a university strength and
an essential experience in training future researchers. Results are broadly available to society and honed by peer review to insure quality. Further down the chain of innovation, industry's "proprietary obsession"
conflicts with the academic need to publish. Basic research is where this
conflict has minimum impact.

Industry would, of course, benefit from technical lead time if a basic
research connection existed. Potentially, a more important factor is that
university basic research should have fewer biases and inhibitions from
precedents of the kind which influence industrial researchers. The product that "didn't make the grade" or the "flawed experiment that failed"
should not dominate university research. This suggests opportunities
for bolder approaches to innovation and support of young (and old) professors with fresh ideas. With inflation at its current level, enormous
progress beyond the *status quo* is necessary in order to justify commercialization of a "new idea." Such progress grows from basic research.

Another essential element is interaction. The linkage must be a functioning connection, not simply a point of contact. The national goal
must be to promote transfer of ideas, mix insights, and accelerate both
the transfer of technology and development. A minimum requirement
for success is that the process have "enthusiastic industrial involvement, fine leadership and management, and excellent research people."[8] Enthusiastic involvement by industry requires a high quality
research program, a role by industry in shaping the program, continued
personal contact, and a monetary commitment by industry large
enough that senior research managers afford it serious attention. In-
timate interpersonal contact is critical. Reading proposed programs or
technical publications is not the most effective means for disseminating
results and simply does not promote a synergistic transfer of ideas and
insights.

Another requirement is patience. It takes time for even a carefully
conceived basic research program to yield new understanding or to
identify a new phenomenon upon which innovation or new technology
can be built. Durable university-industry bridges must be built to be productive. Debate surrounding the federal budget suggests government
does not have the required patience. After all, politics must come first.
For industry, productivity is the "bottom line," and industry is ac-
customed to making long-term investments to this end. It has
demonstrated the required patience so long as the "rules of the game"
are reasonably stable.

Finally, there should be an absolute minimum of federal involvement. Government should support the process of the connection, but

not come between the partners. Government should recognize that it is not the primary user of the results, and therefore should not attempt to steer the science and technology. David[8] and Schacht[9] have noted that government does not have the skills necessary to stimulate technological progress. Even when applicable areas of scientific inquiry are identified, the lack of skills necessary to productively integrate society's needs, as well as the current state of knowledge related to the needs, means most government programs will fail. Industry, on the other hand, has refined these skills because the marketplace and its demand for profit will not tolerate anything else.

Forms of "Connections"

Many proposals have been made to rebuild the connection between industry and the university. As one might expect, they vary in their ability to promote the essential elements of connection.

For example, *philanthropy* is a viable link. It is void of interaction, however, in that little, if anything, is expected in return for some modest level of financial support. It will continue since it services needs other than those under discussion.

Trade associations are another form of the connection between industry and university. The associations collect funds or dues from their members and use the funds to support basic research or generic applied research at universities. At the First Midland Conference on Advances in Chemical Sciences and Technology, sponsored by Dow Chemical Company, Pruitt[10] called for the formation of a Chemical Research Institute to collect industry funds to support long-range chemical research. Stability would probably be its main attribute. Lack of personal interaction between academic and industrial researchers in planning and executing research programs could be a serious flaw. Pruitt's Chemical Research Institute, with difficulty, could be structured to avoid this problem. The difficulty, of course, would stem from an unnecessary function — the redistributor — which, of course, is central to this mechanism. This Institute was established in 1981; it will take some time to calculate its effectiveness.

Another mode of interaction is cooperative research programs. Such research programs involve government, universities, and industry with certain well-defined objectives. One such program which received much national attention was CARP (Cooperative Automotive Research Program), which would have been stewarded by DOT and funded by both industry and government.* High profile programs such as this are federal attempts to steer technology along seemingly desirable paths. Theoretically, well-intentioned federal pressure to work on a common problem will bring academic and industrial researchers together. In practice, however, there are reasons to doubt that this will be successful. Furthermore, forcing massive efforts risks diversion of funds from voluntary and valuable industry-university programs of high mutual interest.

---

*Support for this program was withdrawn by the Reagan Administration.

Another type of mechanism is *mission-oriented institutes.* Here, a university with an outstanding research background and specific expertise performs research for a collection of supporters. At least seven such institutes or centers exist, and more are planned. Support for such institutes and their research programs comes from industry and government, with government's share phasing down if the program succeeds. This type of collective research has the potential for making positive contributions and promoting university-industry cooperation, if attention is paid to the key elements for a successful connection. The MIT-Industry Polymer Processing Program is the most successful example. It now has no federal involvement and a high level of interaction, including all the features discussed earlier. Participants skilfully walk the line between applied and basic research, emphasizing understanding and avoiding proprietary conflicts. Other programs have not been as successful. Many of these programs are experiments of the National Science Foundation. When the results are finally analyzed, they are likely to show at least one major deficiency in the essential connecting elements in every case.

Only true *partnerships* (direct industry funding and close interaction with basic research) capture all essential features of "the connection." Several notable examples exist today. Much has been said about the Monsanto-Harvard connection. Both parties contribute substantially to basic science in the fields of biochemical and biological research through a research partnership. Recognizing the long-term nature of fundamental research, the agreement spans 12 years and involves a substantial $23 million commitment on Monsanto's part. A similar but smaller arrangement has recently been announced involving Exxon and MIT in the field of combustion research; Miles Laboratories has also "connected" with Yale.[11] Yale will rent space in one of its science buildings to Miles, which will set up a biological research institute staffed by Miles scientists. It is likely that Exxon will develop ties to other universities in other areas of science, and that MIT will obtain many more corporate sponsors for basic research. Unfortunately, these examples are the exception rather than the rule; cost plays an important role.

These models have no federal involvement. But there are examples where the federal government does play a role — the right one. It supports the connection. The NSF is supporting research projects carried out jointly by academic and industrial researchers. In this program, government largely leaves selection of the research to industry and academic researchers, hence, the connection is reinforced. The technology is not forced. This is an interesting program and it should be extended. However, it is important to insure that industry plans and capabilities, plus traditional scientific values, are serviced. The intent should be to create true working partnerships. This *caveat* is necessary, because extending this program surely means bringing in mission-oriented agencies such as DOE and DOT. By their very nature, they will overwhelm programs and set their goals, thereby removing much of the usefulness of a reconnection between industry and the universities.

In these examples, solutions to potential barriers of "the connection" have been satisfactorily resolved. Solutions can be found by other partners as well, if they pay attention to the essential elements of a viable coupling. And the effectiveness of the connection will grow if "market forces" are allowed to guide research dollars to the most effective researchers and forms of partnerships. These examples are but a small beginning and are limited to only a few companies and universities. Steps are needed to extend such activities beyond the current participants; many people agree that limited federal support would be an effective means.

Tax Incentives

Money drove industry and universities apart; history suggests it will take financial incentives to bring them together again, at least at the outset. The NSF has recognized this. The NSF-industry joint (matching) funding program, mentioned earlier, is effectively an industry tax incentive to interact with universities in basic research. Industry receives the value of one dollar's worth of research for spending about 25 cents of retained profits. Without NSF support, this would cost 50 cents.

Tax incentives have long been used to stimulate desirable national objectives; interactive basic research should be one such objective. With the present tax treatment of basic research expenses, industry now sees only a small present value for such investments, due to the 20 or more years it may take to see a return. Hence, without some financial inducement, justification for basic research will remain weak. Further, the tax mechanism has many potential advantages. If uniformly applied, tax incentives eliminate the need for bureaucratic judgments and do not create artificial markets. Basic research would thus respond to real needs and demands, rather than to government-created demand. This would provide a built-in incentive for "relevance" which is largely missing today. Tax incentives would encourage participation by a wide range of companies, in many fields, and of all sizes. University research effectiveness would grow as "market forces" guided research dollars to the most effective researchers. Finally, the crucial communications link between basic research and industry would help society benefit from our nation's research efforts.

Two types of incentives have been proposed. Co-funding has been mentioned already. Any co-funding arrangement requires two decisions: one by industry and one by government. This both limits applicability and reduces flexibility. Other, less serious, limits are imposed by the logic of the industrial manager. While co-funding is effectively a tax incentive, it doesn't show on the balance sheet. So, in the NSF example, the industrial research manager gets credit for stewarding only 50 cents of basic research at the cost of 25 cents, which leaves him (and his boss) with the feeling that nothing is different. Another intangible is a general reluctance on the part of some industrial research managers to get involved with government.

Tax credits are another form of incentive. In this case, industry would directly support basic university research, and a portion of the support would be recovered through a tax credit and deduction. This would be an "investment tax" credit for research, an investment in the health and welfare of the nation.

Prager and Omenn[12] imply, based on Canada's experience, that tax incentives will not promote linkages. But Canada's policy is to increase *all* research and development. Credits are available equally for research conducted by industry or by universities. They are clearly not designed to promote specific connections between universities and industry.

Whatever tax incentives are adopted, effective legislation should have certain essential features. The following suggests what these should be, although it is not the intention here to describe specific tax measures or to support any specific legislation:

Size is the most obvious feature. Tax incentives should be significant enough to capture industry's attention. Honeycutt's[13] thesis explored corporate support of university research and its sensitivity to tax incentives by interviewing research managers. He concluded that credits of at least 20-30 percent are needed in order to have a perceptible impact. Bernard and Hess[3] argued before the Advisory Subcommittee on Direct Support of Research and Development, part of President Carter's 1978-79 Domestic Policy Review of industrial innovation, that this level was not sufficient and suggested a 93 percent credit. However one must remember a point mentioned earlier. Financial commitment by any company should be sufficiently large that top management takes notice. As an industry's contribution approaches zero cost dollars, this attention is less likely and a state of low expectation philanthropy could result instead. Deterioration of the working connection could also occur, if it ever developed.

To return to our example, Canada's intentions are different. Canadian tax credits have been increasing since 1975. Since 1979, Canada has had a ten percent (20 percent in depressed areas) tax credit on all research and development operating costs and a 150 percent deduction of expenses exceeding the past three-year average.[14] It is really too early to know if this level of tax incentives is working, but Canadian industry believes that the incentives are insufficient and should be at least 25 percent.[15]

A 25 percent credit in the United States may not be enough to "prime the pump," but could be sufficient to maintain working partnerships once in place. Larger initial incentives may be necessary, with institutionalized provisions to move them back to lower levels over time, depending on the success at building the connections which satisfy national objectives.

A second key feature is that tax incentives should be *uniform*. There should be no attempt to solve special social or political problems with this program. There is no need to single out small versus large businesses for special favor, as suggested by Bernard and Hess.

Next, liberal *carryover provisions* (back and forward) should be included. Firms which are intermittently without tax obligation could take advantage of incentives this way. Smaller firms' earnings often are highly variable; this would protect their interests particularly, though some large corporations would also benefit from this feature.

Duration is another requirement. The tax package should, as a minimum, recognize the lifetime of a student's graduate studies, as well as difficulties of initiation, and generally attempt to provide stability for university programs. This could be done by disallowing benefits to programs of less than three-year duration. However, care should be taken to avoid excesses in the name of stability, since industry and universities should interact in a free market.

An annual *ceiling* is needed on credits available to any one corporation. Some have suggested a limit of five percent of a firm's taxable income. This seems reasonable, but penalizes a firm and the university when the firm does not show a profit. Since research is an investment in the future, such investment should be encouraged even when profits are absent. Perhaps the limit should be the greater of some percentage of taxable income or, alternatively, a smaller percentage of gross sales.

In view of the high price of modern, sophisticated research equipment, credits should apply to the full value of research equipment when this is contributed by a supplier in lieu of cash. This would serve two ends. It would facilitate universities updating their aging facilities. Further, state-of-the-art research equipment would be bait for industry support of partnerships.

Overall, any tax package should be carefully examined both to insure that it clearly supports the connection of industry and universities in their mutual conduct of basic research and to insure that market forces prevail.

Basic University Research: Direct Industrial Support

What is the proper level of direct industrial support? An absolute minimum target is 10-15 percent of all university basic research. In 1980, this would have been about $500 million, about the level suggested by Bernard and Hess and by Herbert Fusfeld.[17] This level would return the percentage of industry's support to the level of the early 1950's.

This notion of an appropriate support level springs from different reasons than those advanced by others who have examined the issue. Fusfeld's goal is to stabilize and strengthen university research, and thus to expand career opportunities for new science and engineering doctorates. His point is that $500 million would support close to 10,000 Ph.D. scientists and engineers, about 40 percent more faculty than today. This would be expected to reverse the "graying" of our faculty researchers. Bernard and Hess hope to increase relevant basic university research by 50-100 percent. ("Relevant," as discussed above, principally embraces the physical and engineering sciences.) This paper, in contrast, focuses on a minimum support level of $500 million, because this amount would make industry a viable "competitor" with the federal agencies supporting basic research today. This figure is about the size of the current DOE basic research program and thus should begin to capture the interest of universities as a financial source worth cultivating. A still higher fraction of industrial support, perhaps one-third or more, is called for if driven by successful, interactive research.

This would portend a change in the role of some government agencies from "redistributors" of general tax funds to, perhaps, stewards of a new system — a concept which needs more definition.

Industry funding should *supplement and complement* federal basic research spending, not totally replace it, since many national objectives would not attract industry attention. In the preferred model, features of which have been developed here, these funding sources would form a national partnership, with the public and private sectors each concentrating in areas of competence, while respecting the roles and responsibilities of the partner.

The national cost for such a program is quite small. On the surface, incremental spending would have a small positive cost depending on the level of tax incentive. For example, if a 25 percent tax credit sparked industry support for 25 percent of total basic research (with government spending constant), lost tax revenues would be about $900 million — less than a quarter of one percent of total federal revenues. A strong case can be made that the return on our nation's research investment, which depends upon the quality of the connection, would over time yield a negative cost to the taxpayer. The cost is small when measured in terms of tax dollars, but the national price of not promoting the connection is immense!

Acknowledgement

The assistance of Dr. R.H. Caulk of my staff in research, critiquing, and developing this paper is gratefully acknowledged.

REFERENCES

1. See, for example, H.D. Doan, "New Arrangements for Industry-Academic Research," *Research Management,* March 1978, p. 33; E.E. David, Jr., "Science Futures: The Industrial Connection," *Science,* March 2, 1979, p. 837; and A.C. Zettlemoyer, "The Industry/Academic Interface," *Chemical and Engineering News,* March 12, 1979, p. 36.

2. National Science Board, *Science Indicators — 1978,* 1979.

3. J.W. Bernard and S.W. Hess, Proposal to the Advisory Subcommittee on Direct Support of Research and Development, Domestic Policy Review of Industrial Innovation, December 7, 1979.

4. R.C. Atkinson, "Tax Incentives and Research," *Science,* May 2, 1979, p. 449.

5. R.M. Sinclair, Private Communication on NSF Overheads, November 28, 1979.

6. P.H. Abelson, "Diversion of Funds from Research," *Science,* April 25, 1980, p. 353.

7. R. Solow, "Technical Change and the Aggregate Production Function," *Review of Economics and Statistics,* 39, (August 1957), p. 312-320.

8. E.E. David, Jr., "General Sarnoff and Generic Research," *Science,* February 15, 1980, p. 719.

9. Committee for Economic Development, *Stimulating Technological Progress,* A Statement by the Research and Policy Committee, January 1980, p. 72.

10. M.E. Pruitt, "A Chemical Industry Proposal," *Proceedings of the First Midland Conference on Advances in Chemical Science and Technology,* October 17, 1979, p. 183.

11. Miles Laboratory, Inc. Press Release, February 8, 1980.

12. D.J. Prager and G.S. Omenn, "Research, Innovation, and University Industry Linkages," *Science,* January 25, 1980, p. 379.

13. J.W. Honeycutt, "Corporate Support of University Research and Its Sensitivity to Tax Incentives," unpublished Masters Thesis, Massachusetts Institute of Technology, June 1978.

14. W.A. MacDonald, Private Communication on Canadian R&D Tax Policies, March 24, 1980.

15. R.C. Scrivener, "Industrial Innovation in Canada, The Need for Incentives," *Research Management,* May 1980, p. 29.

16. H.I. Fusfeld, "The Recent Science and Engineering Doctorate from an Industrial View," Speech at AAAS Symposium on Employment and Advancement Opportunities for Recent Doctorates in Science and Engineering, January 8, 1980.

The Scarcity of Ethical Resources: Strategic Planning for Science

Mark Pastin

Society is prone to make a certain kind of ethical mistake in deciding about actions whose most significant consequences are in the future. We discount these consequences in a way that we reflectively know to be unsound. Decisions about programs of basic research often exemplify this sort of mistake. Moreover, we cannot *directly* correct these mistakes. While the considerations supporting these contentions are abstract and philosophical, specific conclusions can be drawn from them. The no-growth, zero-sum mentality that is currently winning adherents is unethical when viewed within the context of the true importance of the future consequences of our actions. By way of example, the needs of certain private sector entities, such as the recombinant DNA industry and industries dependent on the availability of scarce metals, must receive a higher priority in strategic planning.

Background

The author is in the preliminary stages of a study of strategic science decisions made in the private sector. The specific goal of the study is to understand how the values of enterprise, particularly profitability, interact with the values of science. The subtending goal of the study is to arrive at an applicable procedure for strategic science decisions, a procedure which incorporates ethical factors along with other factors. Such a procedure might be called a procedure for "ethical satisficing" — for choosing the best of the feasible alternatives, where "best" includes an ethical "aspiration level."[1]

The contentions put forth in this paper can be viewed as setting limits on the extent to which such a procedure is possible. While the immediate concern is with a procedure for strategic *science* decisions, the general conclusions apply to any decision procedure which incorporates both ethical and nonethical factors.

This essay grew out of reflection on specific case topics for the study of strategic science decisions and, generally, on the "pause" in productivity in American industry. One case topic is the shift in ownership of

Mark Pastin is Professor of Philosophy and Director for the Center for Private and Public Sector Ethics, Arizona State University.

companies doing recombinant DNA research and the impact this will have on the management and research agendas of these companies. Small companies are being absorbed by large pharmaceutical, energy, and conglomerate firms. Concern about this shift generally focuses on hazards. There has been inadequate consideration of the effects on technological capacity and on the general productivity of American industry. Forecasters compare the technological promise of recombinant DNA research with that of the electronics industry ten years ago. It is worth listening to E.F. Hutton's assessment that "in our opinion, Wall Street is not yet fully aware of the range of applications of recombinant DNA research, namely, that it can be brought to bear on energy, food processing, agriculture, and organic chemicals as well as health care and pharmaceuticals."[2] Thus current ownership changes of the DNA industry must be evaluated in terms of their potential effect upon the promise of this industry — not just in terms of risk.

A second case topic for the broader study is the development of sources of and substitutes for materials for high technology applications. There is evidence that the needs of advanced communications, energy conservation and transportation technologies are not adequately represented in the private sector decisions of suppliers of materials for these technologies. Some suppliers, in response to the political instability of sources in the Soviet Union and South Africa, and in response to the cost of developing substitutes, are diversifying into other businesses. Private industry is not in a position to respond to increasing management of these materials for foreign policy purposes by the Soviet Union. Private sector appeals to place this issue high on the public agenda have not elicited a promising response.[3]

Both case topics involve strategic science decisions which have future consequences that render the decisions unsound — on the assumption the future consequences count as much as immediate consequences.

On a different but related note, it is hard to ignore the "pause" in the productivity of American industry, which is currently receiving so much attention in popular publications. This "pause" probably affects all aspects of American institutional life, but it is best documented for private industry. *Newsweek* begins a special report titled "The Productivity Crisis" with the observation:

> ... lately the rainbow seems to have blurred — or even broken. For the past decade, Americans have watched helplessly as the purchasing power of paychecks has been mercilessly eroded.... No longer do Americans share the great expectations of generations past. For the first time, public opinion polls show that the average U.S. citizen is not at all sure that his children's lot will be better than — or even as good as — his own.[4]

The point of this quote is that U.S. society is, or perceives itself to be, at the peak of a productivity curve, with decline to follow. James Fallows in his "American Industry: What Ails It, How to Save It," strikes the same note.[5] Amitai Etzioni, in the September 1980 Smith-Kline Forum, exhorts us to make quality-of-life sacrifices now as an investment in a quality-of-life society for the future. The question just beneath the surface of this issue is: *Why should we care about a quality-of-life society for the future?* If that is too blunt: How much should we care about the quality of life for the future? This question leads to the ethical issue discussed in this paper.

The Social Discount Rate

That ethical issue is whether or not we are justified in adopting a *Social Discount Rate* (SDR). To adopt a SDR is to discount future costs and benefits, at a fixed percentage per year, just because these costs and benefits accrue in the future. (If there is an annual discount rate of r, then $1 now is worth $1 + r in a year and $1 a year from now is worth $1/1 + r now. So the value of $1 in year n is $1/(1 + r)^n$. This is a simple interest calculation in terms of what must be invested now to return a dollar in year n.) An SDR is often presupposed in policy deliberations. In a popular text on policy formation, the two authors, commenting on Herman Kahn's contention that it is better to spread a fixed amount of genetic damage over several generations, assert that:

> Whether or not we agree with Kahn's ultimate conclusions with respect to nuclear policy, we should probably go along with the contention that you have "done something very useful ... if you can spread the genetic damage over tens of thousands of years." A death in the year 10,000 is not so significant as a death now, and on a less macabre level, a dollar benefit (or cost) in the distant future is of less import than a dollar benefit received today.[6]

The author strongly disagrees with the writers — at least if their comments are taken literally to support an SDR in the sense defined above.

In assessing the case for an SDR, this paper leans on a superb essay by Derek Parfit entitled "Energy Policy and the Further Future."[7] While Parfit concludes, as does this paper, that an SDR is unjustified, in the process of developing his analysis, he presents and perceptively assesses several arguments for an SDR. Four of these arguments are reviewed below; in the process it is possible to collect some key premises for the analysis of this paper.

The first two arguments identify two proper and recognized bases for discounting the future, although they do *not* justify an SDR. The first argument (the *Argument from Probability*) is that since the predicted consequences of our actions are less likely to occur as they extend further into the future, these consequences should count for less than more immediate consequences. It is, of course, true that less probable consequences, no matter when they occur, should count for less than more probable consequences. Parfit offers an example which clearly differentiates futurity and improbability as grounds for discounting:

> Consider predicted deaths from escaped radiation. If we believe in a Social Discount Rate, say one of five percent, we believe that one death next year counts more than a billion deaths in 400 years. On this view it would be morally less important to avoid causing the billion deaths. The Argument from Probability would at most show something very different. We know that, next year, we will have no adequate defense against escape radiation. We may thus be certain that such radiation would, in the near future, cause some deaths. But we may believe that, over the next four centuries, some kind of countermeasure will be invented.... This provides a quite different reason for discounting more remote predicted effects. We would not be

claiming that, if the radiation would be still causing deaths in 400 years, these deaths matter morally a billion times less ... we would be claiming that these remote deaths are a billion times less likely to occur....[8]

In addition, an SDR is not justified as a correction factor for the lower probability of future consequences of actions. While there is *some* correlation between futurity and probability, the correlation is neither exact nor continuous. Predictions for 500 years from now generally are only slightly more probable than those for 750 years from now.

The *Argument from Opportunity Costs* also identifies a proper and recognized base for discounting the future, but fails to justify an SDR. The argument is that immediate consequences should count for more than future consequences, since benefits received now can be reinvested to produce further benefits in the future (so that there is an *opportunity cost* in postponing such benefits). It clearly is appropriate to discount for opportunity cost. But to discount for opportunity cost is not to discount for futurity *per se,* since the correlation between opportunity costs and futurity is approximate at best. For example, some benefits received now (eating an ice cream cone and forgetting it) have no investment value and thus no opportunity cost.

The Argument that our Successors Will Be Better Off supplies a crucial premise for the case argued in this paper. But it, too, fails to justify an SDR. If monetary values are assigned to costs and benefits, the argument simply recognizes a specific kind of decreasing marginal utility. If our successors will be wealthier than we are, we should discount costs and benefits accruing them. An increase or decrease in wealth matters less, the wealthier the recipient. The argument makes sense even if there is no assumption that monetary values can be assigned to the relevant costs and benefits. A given benefit or cost matters less to a person, the greater the person's "level of well-being."

It is right to discount costs and benefits to those who are better off. This principle will figure prominently in later considerations. But this is not to discount for futurity. Given the earlier observation about productivity, the correlation between futurity and well-being or wealth may be indirect rather than direct.

The last of the arguments presented by Parfit which is relevant to the concerns here is the *Argument from Excessive Sacrifice.* This argument contends that, if we do not adopt an SDR, we will be required to make extreme sacrifices to produce small benefits (and avoid small costs) of long duration. Even if we preclude extreme sacrifices for small benefits or costs of long duration, there are, according to the argument, limits to the sacrifices required of us to avoid imposing significant risks of shortages and hazards on future generations. The heart of this argument is the ethical claim that there are limits to the sacrifices that can be required of some on behalf of others, whether or not they presently exist. Supposing that this claim is correct, it does not entail that future costs and benefits count less than present costs and benefits. The claim is that no matter how much future costs and benefits count, there are limits on what can be required of us. And this claim, whether or not it is correct, expresses a deep fact about the human psyche, a fact that strategic science decisions must acknowledge.

Parfit considers two other arguments often thought to support an SDR. Philosophers are concerned about whether or not we have obligations to future generations based on their "special relations" to us. But it is hard to take seriously the idea that what happens to those who will exist matters less if these individuals are not lucky enough to be "specially related" to us. Another argument is that since people generally discount the future, a democratic society is obliged to do the same. But the ethical concern is with what weights future costs and benefits *ought* to have, even if society does not presently recognize them as having these weights. These arguments are clearly in the category of "anything to avoid the consequences" of the unsoundness of an SDR.

A Further Argument for a Modified SDR

These arguments for an SDR do not work. However, there is one further plausible argument for a modified SDR and the argument appeals to *Fairness Across Time.* The argument is that those who will exist would agree with us to adopt an SDR if we and they were "ideally situated" to choose social institutions having differential effects through time. An "ideal situation" would impose a temporal "veil of ignorance"; neither we nor they would know when we would be affected by the institutions. Evidence that we would so agree is provided by the fact that we forgive past generations for the costs they have imposed on us. And, since we dislike being asked to make extreme sacrifices, adoption of an SDR can be viewed as insurance against being required to make such sacrifices on behalf of the future. The flip side of this is that if we turn out to be the unfortunate "futures," our lives might be sacrificed for the comfort of a few "presents." The influence of this worry may be lessened by modifying the discount rate to a Baseline SDR. A Baseline SDR allows discounting of future costs and benefits at a rate of X percent per year *up to a maximum discount of Y percent.* (There are other variations of an SDR, e.g., making it regressive with time, but they do not alter the basic picture.) So the interests of a person who will exist could only be discounted to the fixed maximum percent by those who now exist — a better bet than a straight SDR if we do not know "our time."

Unfortunately, this argument does not work. It clearly does not work for a straight SDR. If the agreement is viewed from the perspective of living at a prosperous time, limiting one's liability to sacrifices for the future is attractive. But if there is the possibility of living without vital resources and at great hazard in any of the futures the agreement might create, one would be looking at a far greater risk of excessive sacrifice than without a discounting agreement.

Reflection also rules out a Baseline SDR. While the people at a given time (e.g., now) could discount one's interests only to 25 percent, if that is the baseline, one would hope that the future is a long time. There is a good chance of existing at a time discounted to the maximum by many generations. One's interest's might be discounted close to 100 percent from the perspective of now, though not by those who now exist. It really is irrational to count one time more than other times, if one doesn't know which time is "his."

An Ethical Satisficing Procedure Without an SDR?

An SDR, modified or unmodified, is unjustified. It does not require great insight to figure out that our interest in the idea of limiting what we can be required to sacrifice for the future is not purely hypothetical. Without an SDR the possibility is strong that "excessive sacrifices" are now required. Should we adopt a principle of limited liability independent of an SDR? At first glance, it seems as if this question, along with more specific questions concerning the strategic use of resources, should be answered within the framework of an applicable and ethically sound procedure for strategic decision-making. While the desired procedure is intended to lead to decisions which are ethically sound, it must also recognize practical constraints on strategic decision-making (limited information, uncertain forecasting models, weak commitments of present management, etc.). So the procedure should elicit decisions which *approximate* ethical ideality within practical constraints.

To develop an applicable ethical decision procedure, one must examine procedures for ethically ideal choice, select components of these which are appropriate for a procedure for strategic decision-making, and formulate these components in an applicable form.

This paper cannot survey the many procedures for ethically ideal choice. All such procedures correct for ethically irrelevant discounting in some way. Irrelevant discounting is the failure to properly weigh certain interests in one's deliberations for ethically unsound reasons. It is not farfetched to identify the inability to be sufficiently sympathetic and empathetic as the fundamental problem of ethics. We have more sympathy for a starving child down the block than for one in Thailand. It is easier (in theory, not in practice) to kill an unseen person than to kill someone eyeball to eyeball. Since the life of the child (or the person killed) counts as much as whether the child is here or in Thailand (and whether the victim is seen or unseen), these facts reflect ethically irrelevant discounting. These are failures of *sympathy,* failures to sufficiently like or dislike what happens to those who are spatially, temporally, racially, or otherwise "distant" from us. Similarly, we find it harder to imagine what it would be like to be an assembly worker or subsistence farmer than to be a professor, consultant, or executive, and so we do not appreciate the costs and benefits of certain jobs. This latter sort of discounting is a failure of *empathy,* a failure to recreate or imagine the circumstances of others when they or their circumstances are "distant" from us. Failures of sympathy and empathy are also the main ingredients of a group of problems, called "social trap" problems, which include the Tragedy of the Commons and the Prisoners' Dilemma.[9] These problems arise in situations in which our interests compete with our ability to sympathize and empathize, so that we thwart not only the interests of our social group, but also our own interests so far as they depend on those of the group.

Procedures for ethically ideal choice correct for irrelevant discounting either by: 1. forcing us into a choice situation in which we identify our interests with the interests we tend to discount; or 2. by specifying conditions optimal for the exercise of our sympathetic and empathetic powers. Neither approach provides the basis for a practical procedure for making strategic decisions which properly assesses future benefits and costs.

The first approach, the Rawlsian, justice-as-fairness approach, attempts to eliminate irrelevant discounting by relying on the self-interested impulses of agents who are shielded from certain information.[10] Fairness is insured by forcing individuals to choose institutions (rules, procedures, laws, social structures) without knowing how they will be affected themselves. The earlier, feigned argument for a Baseline SDR made a claim for temporal fairness insured by having individuals choose an institution, in this case a discount rate, without knowing when they would be affected by it. The conclusion was that choice under conditions of temporal fairness requires excessively large sacrifices on behalf of the future, when this is weighed against the greater harm of not requiring such sacrifices. This is the problem with abstracting a practical procedure from the justice-as-fairness approach. At the level of everyday decisions, we simply will not seriously consider accepting such sacrifices — temporally fair or not. To achieve a moderate level of temporal-fairness, one far short of accepting large sacrifices, the justice-as-fairness approach advises us to choose as if we did not know the time at which we exist. This advice cannot be followed with integrity and be free of self-deception. An individual has no idea how to choose as if one might be living in the years 2080, 2180, or 1980, and one would not be moved even knowing the outcome of this exercise.

The second approach, the moral-sense approach devised by Adam Smith and refined by Roderick Firth, attempts to overcome irrelevant discounting by specifying optimal conditions for the operation of our actual sympathetic and empathetic abilities, our "moral sense."[11] We seek optimal conditions for the operation of our observational senses in scientific contexts, and we may seek optimal conditions for the operation of our "moral sense" in contexts of ethical choice. Optimal conditions for the operation of sympathetic and empathetic abilities resemble (and are the basis of) those optimal for judgment in a court of law. The conditions may include having direct experience of one's own interests, seeking all the facts relevant to a choice, being aware of one's prejudices, and being impartial. The "moral sense" approach has an advantage as a model for an applicable procedure; it is motivational. If we make choices in circumstances in which we are truly sympathetic and empathetic with those affected, it is natural not to discount their interests.

The problem with this approach is that though it sharpens the actual abilities of human beings to be sympathetic and empathetic, there are limits inherent in us as creatures. There are circumstances in which our "moral senses" are sufficiently sharp that we make sound decisions concerning presently existing individuals who are physically, occupationally, or racially "distant." But we are not equally likely or able to care about or recreate the situations of people who *will* exist. This shows in our differential attitude, even with "moral senses" sharpened, to sacrifices required on behalf of existing individuals, versus sacrifices required on behalf of the future. It is commonly, if not universally, con-

ceded that large sacrifices are required of us in demanding present circumstances (to prevent a rape or murder), but there is no sense that we
must make such sacrifices on behalf of the future. This difference
precisely expresses our adherence to an ethically unsound SDR. Given
our own limitations, we cannot compensate for ethically unsound discounting of the future by adhering to a corrective decision procedure.
To admit that our own abilities are limited in such a way that we cannot
expect to make ethically sound strategic decisions is neither to condone
nor to condemn ethically unsound decisions. It is to acknowledge the
facts. Unless we acknowledge the facts, we can do nothing to develop
strategies and policies to compensate for the shortcomings of individual
decision-makers.

The Prescription

It is time to pull some of the strands of this essay together. The paper
has argued that an SDR is not justified, that the future consequences of
our actions count as much as immediate consequences do. But there is
no way to make future consequences count as much as immediate consequences in actual strategic decision-making. The gravity of these conclusions is increased by the fact that we are in the midst of collectively
deciding to trade the interests of those who will be for interests of those
who are. Some of the points raised in reviewing arguments for an SDR
help unravel this knot. Two important principles were elicited in the process. The first is that *costs and benefits are less important in direct proportion to the level of well-being of those who receive them.* The second principle is that *we ought to accept benefits now if there is an opportunity cost
in delaying,* i.e., if we lose the opportunity to produce a greater benefit
by delaying.

The practical pay-off of the first principle is this: if we are not going to
make substantial sacrifices on behalf of the future, and if what happens
then is as important as what happens now, we are ethically obliged to
pursue courses of action which make the recipients of the consequences
of our actions better off. There are, we noted earlier, two conceptions of
the goal of making people better off — increasing their well-being in
specifically monetarily terms, or increasing their well-being in broader
terms. This paper advocates pursuing the goal of both the narrower and
the broader conceptions. The narrowly conceived goal, increasing
wealth, can be pursued with only a limited likelihood of success. We are
not going to make huge sacrifices to substantially increase the wealth of
our successors. Even if we did, increasing the wealth of our near successors — which is the most that we can plausibly expect to accomplish
— is not a significant benefit, viewed in the time frame over which the
costs we now generate may be felt. There is more promise in pursuing
the goal of increasing well-being, where "well-being" is construed more
broadly. But how is "well-being" to be understood more broadly? We
should think not only of improving the quality of life, but also of empowering future generations. Empowering does not mean improving
the material circumstances of future generations, but rather increasing
the ability of future generations to produce a life of quality from
whatever circumstances we leave for them.

This brings us to the second principle elicited in discussing an SDR, the principle that we ought to accept benefits now if there is an opportunity cost in delaying. This principle supports the strategy derived from the first principle, provided that we count abilities as benefits, whether or not the abilities are actually exercised to produce a good quality of life. The objective, then, is to put future generations in a position to live lives of quality. There is no guarantee that the position will be well exercised. The strategy is familiar in contemporary terms; we know that technology transfer, which is empowering, is often more appropriate than direct support, which may not be at all empowering.

So the prescription is that we correct for our ethically irrelevant discounting of the future by embracing the task of increasing our productivity, not only to hand over a healthy industrial machine to the next generation, but also to hand over the ability to confront new and troublesome circumstances. There is good evidence that this need not be unpleasant or a sacrifice for us. After all, we do not measurably empower future generations by saving a drop of oil or working a second job. We empower future generations by planning intelligently and thinking creatively. This, of course, is the strategy for a rapid growth economy.

The essay by James Fallows, mentioned above, and other recent analyses of what ails American industry point to the Silicon Valley electronics industry as a bright star in the gloomy sky. If there is a salient factor in the success of the stronger Silicon Valley firms, it is that they outspend their competition in R&D. This is not a novel approach, but it is the right approach. Paul Samuelson, commenting on the productivity crisis, says

> America is a slow-investing economy, and our support for technological and scientific innovation has been declining. *Capital* and *knowledge* are the prime sources of productivity and growth — not Washington hot air about "supply-side economics."[12]

The point is that there is a definite *ethical* imperative to increase the commitment to R&D in the private sector. This is the only way for us to treat future generations fairly, given the plain facts that we will not make excessive sacrifices, that our moral sensitivity to the temporally distant is limited, and that we cannot appeal to an SDR to justify our lack of sensitivity.

This prescription has consequences for specific cases and issues. To take one example, investment in the recombinant DNA industry ought to be encouraged, and it is important that companies engaged in such research develop independently enough of their own management strategies and research agendas, on the model of the Silicon Valley companies. But the recombinant DNA industry also threatens to impose incredible risks on future generations. We could argue about the level of risk actually imposed. However, if we do think not in terms of costs and benefits directly accruing to future generations, but in terms of empowering future generations, these risks are much more justified. There is no question that recombinant DNA research is extremely promising from the perspective of providing tools to later generations. It is not that society should ignore risks to future generations. But, it should accept much greater risks with respect to empowering technologies than it accepts for the production of present or temporally near benefits. It is a good bet that society will impose great risks in any case. Better that they be imposed in areas which can produce distinct empowering benefits.

Society must also support more mature high technology industries. In concrete terms, this means that steps must be taken to assure satisfaction of the material preconditions of health in these industries, such as the availability of critical metals. The problem is not just that supplies of these metals are limited; the supplies are located mainly in the Soviet Union and South Africa, and the Soviet Union has shown a markedly increased interest in managing its metal resources for foreign policy objectives in recent years. Further, current suppliers of these metals are diversifying into other areas, rather than facing the political instability of sources and the high costs of developing substitutes for the metals. This is not to bang the drum for government-business cooperation "on the Japanese model," whatever that is. The problem raised here poses the challenge, important for the twenty-first century, of incorporating management of international social and political issues in present strategic planning and in the practice of management.[13] The best approach may be to have the government look after the interests of industries when their welfare is politically dependent. The trap in this is that this will mean virtually all industries in the near future. It is also essential to create incentives for private management to incorporate these social and political variables in their strategic planning. This is not the place to argue for specific programs of incentives.[14]

Conclusion

It may appear perverse for an ethicist to argue, firstly, that society cannot discount future consequences of its actions on the basis of their futurity, and secondly, that given society's moral limitations, the best course of action is to promote the interests of future generations by increasing current productivity — even at great risk to those who will exist. The argument is that the *best* society *will* do is to make future generations better off, in the sense of being more able to meet the challenges of their circumstances. The perversity of this recommendation lies in the fact that it would involve little current cost, and would produce great profit for many. The simple truth is that, although the much recommended strategy of excessive sacrifice is respectable in the moral tradition of mortification of the flesh, it is not a workable strategy for achieving fairness to the future. And, that, not moral respectability, ought to be the goal.

REFERENCES

1. The reference, of course, is to the work of Herbert Simon on "satisficing." The classic discussion is Simon's *Administrative Behavior,* 3rd edition (New York, 1976). The idea is that managers do not, and cannot optimize, in actual practice. Instead, they seek decisions which enable them to achieve results up to an "aspiration level," which is a minimum acceptable result along some

dimension. While satisficing theory is sometimes emphatically described as non-normative, it does not violate the intentions of the theory to abstract a procedure for achieving various aspiration levels, including an ethical aspiration level, in actual decision-making.

2. The quote is attributed to Nelson Schneider of E.F. Hutton in *News for Investors*, Vol. VII, No. 3 (March 1980), p. 60.

3. Herbert E. Meyer, "Russia's Sudden Reach for Raw Materials," *Fortune,* July 28, 1980, pp. 43-44.

4. *Newsweek,* September 8, 1980, p. 50.

5. *Atlantic Monthly,* September 1980, pp. 35-50.

6. Richard Zeckhauser and Elmer Schaefer, "Public Policy and Normative Economic Theory," in *The Study of Policy Formation,* ed. by Raymond Bauer and Kenneth Gergen (New York; Free Press, 1968), p. 85. See pp. 84-92 for a good general discussion of optimization over time.

7. Published by the Center for Philosophy and Public Policy, University of Maryland, 1981.

8. *Ibid,* p. 4.

9. On social trap problems see John Platt's "Social Traps," *American Psychologist,* August 1973, pp. 641-651, and Thomas C. Schelling's *Micromotives and Macrobehavior* (New York; Norton, 1978). On the Tragedy of the Commons, see Garrett Hardin's classic "The Tragedy of the Commons," *Science,* Vol. 162, No. 1243 (1968). Any book on game theory tells the story of the Prisoners' Dilemma.

10. The reference is to the view of justice espoused by John Rawls in his now classic *A Theory of Justice* (Cambridge, Massachusetts; Belknap Press, 1971).

11. Adam Smith developed his famous theory of the "moral sense" in his *The Theory of the Moral Sentiments* (the sixth edition of 1790 is definitive). It is worth observing that the Adam Smith of *The Moral Sentiments* is the same as the Adam Smith of *The Wealth of Nations,* an often ignored fact. Roderick Firth's perspicuous development of a contemporary moral sense theory is presented in "Ethical Absolutism and the Ideal Observer," *Philosophy and Phenomenological Research* (March 1952) and reprinted in *Readings in Ethical Theory,* 2nd ed., ed. by Wilfrid Sellars and John Hospers (New York, 1970).

12. *Newsweek,* September 8, 1980, p. 68.

13. H.J. Zoffer, in a report of the conclusions of an Association of Colleges of Business Administration international project on management in the twenty-first century, emphasizes that this challenge must appear on *current* agendas. This report by Zoffer, Dean of the Graduate School of Business Administration at the University of Pittsburgh, has not yet been published.

14. This issue is the topic of my "Strategic Planning: Social and Ethical Issues" (manuscript). Specific disincentives that should be removed are discussed in Pastin and Hooker, "Ethics and the Foreign Corrupt Practices Act," *Business Horizons* (December 1980), pp. 43-47.

New Academic Positions: The Outlook in Europe and North America*

Charles V. Kidd

Universities in the United States will offer few new academic positions during the 1980's. This creates the prospect that the vigor of basic science will decline unless there is a sustained flow of young persons into academic science. Similar problems exist in Sweden, the Federal Republic of Germany, Denmark, Norway, France, the United Kingdom, Canada, Japan, the Soviet Union, and perhaps in other countries. The current and prospective difficulties have given rise to analyses, proposals for action, and some actual programs.[1] Aspects of the situation in some of these countries and of the measures that they have taken are pertinent to the United States.

Research, Enrollment Growth Rates, and Academic Jobs

During the 1960's, all Western industrialized countries rapidly increased support for university research in the natural sciences and engineering. Between 1968 and 1972, these countries experienced a slowdown or "a declining beginning."[2]

University enrollments have followed the same trend as university research support — rapid increases and then a decline of the rate of increase.[3] Funds for university operating costs are strongly influenced in all countries by levels of enrollment, universities being regarded at the political level primarily as teaching institutions. A substantial part of the cost of academic science is paid for out of the general operating funds, mostly in the form of salaries paid to faculty members who are engaged in both research and teaching. Funds available for academic science and for faculty positions are therefore strongly influenced by enrollment trends.

The reduction in the rate of expansion of enrollments, combined with the slow-down in the growth of research expenditures, will sharply reduce the number of new academic jobs. The number of new jobs can shrink even while enrollment and research expenditures are still rising.

Charles V. Kidd is Research Professor of Public Affairs at George Washington University.

This will happen not only in universities but also in any research organization that experiences a rapid rate of growth, followed by a slower growth rate or a decline. Indeed, the number of new jobs in academic science has dropped markedly in virtually all Western countries (Table 1) since the 1960's, when rapidly increasing undergraduate

TABLE 1. Average annual growth rates of full-time university faculty from 1965 to 1977 in five Western countries.

Country	Faculty growth rate (percent)			
	1961 to 1965	1965 to 1969	1969 to 1973	1973 to 1977
United Kingdom	13	6	4	1
United States	13	10	3	4
Germany	23	12	11	1
Canada	17	20	7	2

and graduate enrollment and rapidly rising budgets for academic science produced an unprecedented demand for college and university teachers in all disciplines. In Germany, for example, faculty positions increased by 23 percent a year from 1961 to 1965. The comparable figures for the United Kingdom and the United States were 13 percent, and for Canada 17 percent. Then, beginning in the early 1970's, as the rates of increase in both enrollments and expenditures declined, there was a sharp drop in the demand for young academics. By the late 1970's the growth rate of faculties had dropped to 1 to 4 percent per year.[4]

As a consequence of the large-scale hiring of faculty in the 1960's, most universities have an abnormally high proportion of young faculty members (Table 2). [Normal is defined as the age distribution in a steady-state system[5] with a constant number of undergraduates and reasonable assumptions as to mobility, retirement age, and mortality.]

TABLE 2. Proportion of faculty in two age brackets in various countries in 1977 and the steady-state distribution. [Data from (5, 25)]

Country	Proportion of faculty	
	31 to 45 years old	51 to 65 years old
France	64	11
Germany	59	14
Great Britain	54	17
United States	57	20
Canada	62	15
Steady state	46	25

This bulge, although aging year by year, will remain in the national systems for 20 to 30 more years. At the same time, the abnormally low proportion of faculty members at the upper end of the age scale, the 51- to 60-year-old age bracket (Table 2), will mean that relatively few vacancies will be created by retirements during the next 5 to 15 years. In addition, the earlier hiring bulge provided positions to some persons who would have had difficulty in competing successfully either before or after the period of rapid increases in enrollments. In all countries, most of those hired during the 1960's have a high degree of job security because of contractual agreements (tenure), civil service status, job protection laws, or some combination of the three.

Low Future Growth Rates

The continuing consequences of the declines in rates of increase in both university enrollments and research expenditures will be augmented or moderated by future changes. The future may bring surprises, but in no country, with the possible exception of Japan, is it now considered realistic to assume resumption of the growth that characterized the 1960 to 1970 period.

The outlook for university enrollment varies widely. One factor influencing enrollment is simply the number of persons entering the traditional university age bracket, and this varies among countries. In the United States and Canada, a 20 percent decline in the 18-year-old cohort began in 1980 and will recover somewhat after 1990. In Germany, the United Kingdom, and the Netherlands, the 18-year-old cohort will grow until 1985 and then decline precipitously for a decade; the drop in Germany will be more sudden and deeper than in any other Western country. In Sweden, Norway, and France, the 18-year-old cohort will remain at or above the 1975 level until 1990 and then drop moderately until 1995.

While the United States and particularly Canada are concerned over the consequences of the decline in the 18-year-old group, Germany, the Netherlands, and the United Kingdom worry about how to accommodate over the next few years what the Germans call "the student mountain" and the English call "the student hump." Despite the prospect for sustained rates of enrollment growth, these countries will nevertheless have few new academic positions over the next few years. In Sweden, Norway, and France, there will be a few new academic jobs, but future enrollment changes are not expected to aggravate the serious effects of the decline in rates of growth of research support and enrollment.

Declines in growth rates and prospective changes in research support levels and enrollments play different roles in these countries, but the outlook for new academic positions is fairly uniform and has led to the proposal or adoption of a variety of national programs.

Germany

The Science Council (Wissenschaftsrat) recognized in 1975 that new academic positions would be created only at the rate of about 1 percent a year for about a decade. The alarming outlook led the council, together with other major scientific and academic organizations, to urge that a special program be established to hold outstanding young scientists in academic life until permanent posts become available with the retirement at age 60 of large numbers of those hired in the 1960's.[6] This program, the Heisenberg Program for the Development of Young Scientific Talent, was ratified by the federal government and the states (Lander) on 4 November 1977. The initial intent was to provide 150 10-year fellowships in each of the 5 years from 1978 through 1982.

Responsibility for administering the program was given to the Deutsche Forschungsgemeinschaft (DFG), the independent German research association,[7] which set up a special body to establish guidelines for the program.[8] This group decided to insist on high academic qualifications, even if this meant the award of fewer stipends than originally planned. The guidelines limited competition to those formally declared eligible to teach and carry on research in universities, and a maximum age of 33 was set. Those in all fields of science and the humanities (the traditional scope of German Wissenschaft) were eligible to compete. The stipend level was set at about $24,000 a year, a generous level for a fellowship but a modest salary for an outstanding young academic. Finally, negotiations with governments resulted in reduction of the term of the awards from 10 to 15 years.

There were only 484 applicants during the first 2 years of the program, even though the age limit was relaxed. The budget provided funds for 300 stipends, but the selection board decided that only 144 applicants were qualified. The successful applicants were divided among broad fields as follows: humanities and social science, 33 percent; biomedical sciences, 27 percent; physical sciences and mathematics, 37 percent; engineering, 3 percent.

The average quality of applicants, as well as the number, was lower than expected, perhaps because the program was new and not well known. Also, some academic positions were still available; in fact, 27 of the 144 successful stipendiaries resigned during the first 2 years of the program, most to take permanent academic positions. In addition, a new federal law provides that a negotiated proportion of professors should be given the status of civil servants (tenure in U.S. terms) provided that staffing requirements exist and the state budgets are adequate.[9] In this situation, the nontenured university teacher-investigators who were best qualified and hence most likely to be given tenure under the law stayed at their university posts. Finally, some potential applicants apparently saw themselves faced with unemployment after expiration of the 5-year stipend or with incomes that would lag behind those of their colleagues with regular university jobs.

In spite of these initial problems, the DFG has announced that the program will remain in place and be expanded. Whether expenditures will increase from the $8 million spent in 1979 to the $27 million envisioned for 1982 remains to be seen.[10]

In addition to the Heisenberg Program, the Arbeitsgemeinschaft der Grossforschungseinrichtungen (AGF), the association of big science establishments, has proposed that 800 new positions be created in the large research establishments over the next few years and that the AGF eliminate the posts when retirements create vacancies on a large scale late in the 1980's. The Ministry of Science and Technology has approved this proposal in principle. Another program, the so-called Fiebiger Program, proposed by the German Rector's Conference, would link the creation of university posts to increases in enrollment. Since enrollments are expected to increase for a number of years, the proposal would provide for continuing growth of faculty. Then, when enrollments decline and retirements begin on a large scale, the positions vacated would be eliminated, and the system would have a reasonable age distribution. This plan is unlikely to be financed, at least at the proposed level, primarily because the federal and state ministries of finance are unconvinced that any positions vacated by retirees would actually be eliminated.

The United Kingdom

The Science Research Council,[11] the governmental body in the United Kingdom with primary responsibility for academic science, has noted:

> The almost complete absence of expansion of universities in recent years, coupled with the age distribution within the academic profession — itself a consequence of the rapid expansion of the sixties — has discouraged many potentially high calibre research workers from proceeding to post-doctoral work.

The Medical Research Council has stressed the fact that government laboratories, which perform a larger proportion of basic research than is the case in the United States, face a similar problem.[12] The United Kingdom has established two modest programs to deal with these problems. First, the Science Research Council awards advanced fellowships to carefully selected scientists, under 35 years of age, who are well qualified for academic careers but do not yet hold tenured posts. The awards are made for periods of up to 5 years. The purpose and the terms of the program are similar to the German Heisenberg Program and to Canadian programs described below. Applications for these fellowships declined from 251 in 1977 to 48 in 1979, apparently because young people are not enthusiastic over such short-term arrangements. Awards over the same period declined from 33 to 19, a reflection of a decline in the quality of the applicants.

Second, the Science Research Council decided in November 1979 to establish a Special Replacement Fellowship Scheme, under which a small number of outstanding senior research scientists may be released from tenured university positions and formal teaching responsibilities to concentrate full-time on research. At the same time, the university would agree to make an additional tenured position available to a young faculty member, chosen in the usual way by the university, in any scientific or engineering field supported by the Science Research Council. Ten awards were to be made in the fall of 1980, 15 in 1981, and 10 in each of the subsequent 3 years. As planned, the program would cost approximately $3 million. The number of awards, however, will be influenced by the funds made available to the Science Research Council by the government.

These experimental programs are small for a number of reasons. Neither the research councils, the universities, nor the proposed beneficiaries are certain how much these programs will contribute to solving the problem, even if generously financed. In addition, a difficult national economic situation and the philosophy of the Conservative government may inhibit proposals that involve substantial additional expenditures. Finally, universities have more general financial difficulties, and the fellowship programs must compete for attention and money with other issues: research policy problems involving an impending change in the traditional dual system of support of universities, a shift to greater selectivity in support of universities, the need to strengthen links between industry and universities, and managing the balance between big science and little science.

France

In France the major institutional homes for research are governmental laboratories. These include the extensive network of laboratories of the Centre National de la Recherche Scientifique (CNRS), many of which are associated with, but not a part of, universities. Other nationally financed, staffed, and operated laboratories exist in such fields as health [Institut National de la Sante et de la Recherche Medicale (INSERM)], atomic energy (Commissariat a l'Energie Atomique), and agriculture [Institut National de la Recherche Agronomique (INRA)]. Universities and the elite national technical institutions (the *grandes ecoles*) pay the salaries of faculty members who teach and conduct research, but most research by university faculty members is conducted in the associated laboratories. The government has tended to express its concern for the health of basic research mainly through measures to strengthen the government laboratories. One aspect of concern was expressed in an influential report:[13]

> Investigators were recruited in large numbers between 1960 and 1968. Today, the average age of CNRS investigators is 40 years — a relatively young group. The shape of the age pyramid is such that substantial blocking of promotion can be foreseen until 1990.

France's approach is different from that of Germany, the United Kingdom, and Canada. France has decided to increase the number of permanent positions in government laboratories (primarily CNRS and INSERM) by 3 percent a year, even though this reduces the funds available for research in budgets that are already tight. National budgets provide specific sums and specified numbers of new positions by agency. In 1980, 370 new research positions and 698 new supporting positions (engineers and technicians) were created at an initial annual cost of about $13 million.[14]

Other steps taken to speed the entry of young researchers into the government laboratories include the introduction of a uniform 4-year probationary period instead of an indefinite one and the gradual reduction of the age of appointment to permanent posts.[15] These two measures increase the number of persons at the lowest grade who are eligible for promotion. Later, as more people become eligible for successively higher permanent posts, more jobs at the higher levels will be funded.

The government is also trying to encourage more exchange between laboratories and universities. Positions in the laboratories are being made more closely equivalent in pay and prerequisites to the corresponding positions in universities, and the government has stated that scientists have an obligation to move between governmental laboratories and universities.

These changes have generated opposition among those affected, who claim that they were not adequately consulted. Some point out that mobility between laboratories and universities is stated as an obligation of employees but that the system does not provide positive incentives for mobility. Others note that many of those who serve the 4-year probationary period will not be appointed to permanent posts. For the most part, the protests reflect the high value placed on equity and security by employees, and the position of the government reflects the priority it gives to efficiency, productivity through selection by merit, and promotion on the basis of achievement.

At the universities, even fewer new positions have been available than at the government laboratories, essentially because the rate of growth of universities was greater and the cessation of growth came more quickly:[16]

> The number of permanent posts has been increasing in both industry and the public establishments, but in universities there was a severe reduction in new posts.... Only 275 new teaching-research posts were created in the universities in 1976 — only about 1.0 percent of the total of posts. This is much below the 3 percent rate for the public establishments.

The Ministry of the Universities proposed that a fixed number of new academic posts be created annually, but the Ministry of Finance has not approved such a plan. The government, however, promoted several thousand of those already in the system to newly created positions, an action that will decrease further the possibility of adding new positions for young persons.

The markedly more favorable treatment of staff in the government laboratories is attributable to a number of factors: repercussions at the universities from the 1968 disruptions, the strong power base of the research function in the national government, and the large financial burden that would be generated by creating a substantial number of faculty positions. The net effect of all these factors is to make the prospect for new university positions rather dim.

Canada

The Natural Sciences and Engineering Research Council of Canada (NSERC), the central government agency for funding academic research in science and engineering, has called attention to the serious adverse effects on basic research of declining rates of increases in R & D expenditures and in university enrollments.[17] The Science Council of Canada, a semiautonomous group that provides an independent point of view on science policy, has also sounded a warning.[18] Both organizations reviewed the outlook for research in the natural sciences and engineering in Canada and made recommendations.

The Science Council concentrated on manpower measures, advocating such steps as *1.* improving pension portability, *2.* granting special status to outstanding older university staff members to encourage them to continue research, *3.* establishing special university research chairs in the provinces in fields of special interest to them, and *4.* encouraging university staff to spend a year in industry. The 5-year plan of the NSERC is more ambitious, advocating measures to elevate total national R & D expenditures sharply as a percentage of gross national product in order to deal with the obsolescence of research instruments, increase the effectiveness of university-industrial relations, attain a more reasonable regional balance in research, and expand targeted research, while also maintaining a strong foundation of free research.

To sustain a flow of young scientists into the academic system, the central recommendation of the NSERC, which endorsed the measures proposed by the Science Council, was to establish a new program of University Research Fellowships. Awards would be made to outstanding young researchers for 3 years, with 2-year renewals available and the possibility of a second 5-year award for up to 50 percent of the recipients. The applicants would hold all university privileges of an assistant professor (except full tenure) and would be eligible to apply for NSERC research grants. The purpose is "to retain some of the excellent researchers as the nucleus of the new generation of Canadian professors that will be required for the 1990's".[17] During the summer of 1980, there were 385 applications for the new fellowships and 100 fellowships were awarded. The intent is to award about 100 fellowships in each of the next 4 years. The first year's cost will approximate $3 million.

United States

Over the last few years in the United States a number of developments constitute a *de facto* but unplanned and unheralded beginning of adaptation to the prospect of few new permanent academic positions. One device, used in various forms in all countries, is to hire people on short-term or indefinite contracts and without the status and benefits of faculty members (for example, the protection of unemployment security laws in Europe). The most widely used variation of indefinite employment status in the United States is the nonfaculty postdoctoral position. In 1978 there were about 4000 nonfaculty postdoctoral research staff in science and engineering in U.S. universities. The group is growing about 2½ times as rapidly as faculty.[19] These new research positions do not depend on university enrollments and usually do not involve teaching. They also tend to create an unequitable two-class society.

Another form of adaptation is the continuing formation of extradepartmental research laboratories, institutes, and programs that also do not depend on enrollment, and that may or may not provide faculty for teaching. For example, the National Institutes of Health now support almost 700 university-based research centers for the medical sciences, at a cost of about $350 million a year.

There is a widespread belief, however, that such spontaneous forms of adjustment may be inadequate. Reports analyzing trends and proposing action have been prepared, among them a Carnegie Council report.[20] and public officials and various organizations have advocated a number of lines of action. A committee of the National Research Council, the operating arm of the National Academy of Sciences, has advocated a plan almost identical to the United Kingdom's special replacement fellowship program, except for greater emphasis on differences in the job outlook among fields. The National Science Board, the governing body of the National Science Foundation, has considered various kinds of fellowships and postdoctoral awards designed to hold a small number of outstanding investigators in academic science until permanent jobs open up. Others have advocated new kinds of structural adjustments. For example, Frank Press.[21] science and technology adviser to President Carter, suggested the establishment of national centers for research:

> A number of university science departments might be designated as National Research Centers. Such Centers might receive coherent area grants for 3- to 5-year periods from government agencies, but many projects in them would be judged individually and competitively. They would be staffed primarily by recent Ph.D.'s supported full time by government grants, with the universities offering rolling 3-year periods of tenure and space and other amenities to make the positions attractive. Faculty members in departments might become researchers at the centers for periods of 1 to 3 years and vice versa. These Centers would enable universities to bring young scientists into the university community, in close connection with established departments. In this way, it would ensure the flow of the best young minds into the basic research structure of the universities.

Richard Atkinson,[22] former director of the National Science Foundation, made these suggestions:

> There are several areas where government assistance might play a role. Programs to facilitate mid-career shifts for tenured faculty interested in striking out in new directions might open positions for younger Ph.D.'s. The government could contribute at least a portion of the funds necessary to maintain a retirement plan in effect, and only on condition that the vacated position is made available to a younger person. A second possibility might be a program of Senior Research Scientist Grants for outstanding scientists ... to permit them to devote more time to research. Meantime, the university would use the released salary to appoint a young faculty member. A third idea is the encouragement of joint university-industry research institutes which would be housed at the university and under university auspices.

Some analysts, however, question the desirability of federal action. Klitgaard[23] described the most significant reservations.

1. Individual scientists and universities tend to believe that during periods when funds are limited, the quality of academic science may be sustained more effectively by strong support through existing channels, than by special governmental programs designed to provide new positions. Indeed, the executive agencies themselves have not been willing

to include specific proposals in budgets submitted to Congress, and there has been no public objection to this omission from the scientific community or from universities.

2. Universities tend to shy away from federal programs that interject the government, even indirectly, into personnel decisions.

3. Spontaneous adjustment and market forces will result in a reasonable flow of young investigators into the various research sectors, including academic science.

4. Movement of a large share of talented scientists and engineers into nonacademic careers can have many positive consequences for them, for the economy, and for the society.

5. A large component of the problem is the high proportion of university faculty with tenure, and modification of tenure practices involves not the federal government, but the parties to the private contract, universities and individuals.

6. Most assessments of the effects of a declining 18-year-old group on university enrollments did not differentiate among types of higher education institutions. Enrollment will almost certainly not decline at the major universities where most academic research is carried on.

7. It is not clear that there will be as few new jobs as earlier analyses indicated, or that the period of job scarcity will last as long as was projected.

These reservations may or may not prove to be valid. In any case, it appears certain that discussion will continue about the most appropriate action to take in the face of shortages of academic jobs, the effects of which are not forseeable.

Conclusion

Experience in other countries may be valuable in assessing the actions contemplated in the United States to respond to consequences of the shortage of new academic positions.

The most direct action on a significant scale has been taken by France, where new permanent jobs in government laboratories are being created at the rate of 3 percent a year. Neither in Canada, Germany, nor the United Kingdom have additional permanent positions been created in universities.

The devices designed to keep young scientists available until retirements make permanent jobs available in universities (the Heisenberg Program in Germany, the Special Replacement Fellowship Scheme in the United Kingdom, and the University Research Fellowships in Canada) are experimental and are operating on a small scale. Experience in both Germany and the United Kingdom suggests that unanticipated developments, such as changes in the job market, may be expected, and that it is wise to begin programs on a small scale. Further, most of the programs that are in place do not appear to provide support long enough to cover the full anticipated period of shortages of permanent positions. This is a warning signal that the plans as initially put into effect may not meet the stated objectives.

Both short- and long-run forecasts of such matters as enrollment levels, new academic jobs, industrial employment scientists, and numbers of advanced degree holders have proved to be fallible in all countries. Any actions taken should not be based on the assumption that such forecasts are precise.[24]

There is greater emphasis on government action to promote mobility in Europe than in the United States, not because mobility is considered more important in Europe, but because the barriers to mobility are greater there.

The shortage of academic jobs is seen in all countries not as an isolated phenomenon but as part of a complex of science policy issues. Some countries have adopted specific measures to deal with the scarcity of new academic jobs, but all face broader and more urgent problems related to science policy, and the measures they are taking have been put in this context. The goal of any action taken in the United States should be stated not only in terms of sustaining the vitality of academic science as traditionally organized, but also in terms of providing new institutional forms (within, attached to, or separate from universities) as sites for basic research and as sites for jobs for young investigators. These avenues have been explored in other countries in ways which differ in many respects from the United States.

Finally, the actions described in this paper may be insufficient to provide enough new jobs in those countries where strong forces are leading to particularly sharp reductions in the number of new positions in basic or academic research. This suggests the importance of general measures designed to sustain the vitality of national basic research systems when there are few new posts. Such measures include organizing research teams better, improving communications among various parts of research systems, increasing mobility within the research system, enhancing the relevance of academic science to the solution of national problems while sustaining a good environment for basic science, inaugurating special efforts to exploit emerging scientific fields, and minimizing the bureaucratization of academic science. Attention is paid to such measures as a matter of course in all countries but with varying degrees of effectiveness. The scarcity of new academic positions is simply one additional reason for concentrating on increasing the productivity of science.

REFERENCES

1. European Science Foundation, *Employment Prospects and Mobility of Scientists in Europe* (Strasbourg, France, in press).

2. Committee for Scientific and Technological Policy, Organization for Economic Cooperation and Development, *Trends in R&D in the Higher Education Sector in OECD Member Countries Since 1965 and Their Impact on National Basic Research Efforts* (Paris, 1979).

3. United Nations Educational, Scientific and Cultural Organization, *Statistical Yearbook* (Paris, 1963 and 1977).

4. For information on slowdowns in other countries, see:
   Soviet Union
   L.E. Nolting and M. Feschbach, in *Science*, February 1, 1980, p. 496.
   T. Gustafson in *The Social Context of Soviet Science*, L.L. Lubrano and S.G. Solomon, eds. (Boulder, Co.: Westview Press, 1980), p. 41.

Australia

N. Crequer, *Times Educational Supplement,* December 14, 1979, p. 26.
Denmark

K. Jensen, *Notes on Ageing of the Scientific Personnel in the University Sector in Denmark* (Copenhagen: Danish Council for Scientific Personnel and Planning, 1979).
Norway

19. National Sciences and Engineering Research Council of Canada, *op. cit.,* p. 61.

E. Fjellbirkeland, personal communication.
Japan

F. Kodama, "S&T Policy Outlook: Main Trends and Issues; Japan Case Study," paper prepared for Directorate for Science, Technology and Industry, OECD (Saitama, Japan: Saitama University, 1980).
Sweden

R. Svennson, "The Prospects for New Academic Positions in Sweden," unpublished memorandum, Swedish Council for Planning and Coordination of Research, November 10, 1979.

W. Barnaby, *Nature* 283, 1980, 615.

5. National Research Council, *Research Excellence Through the Year 2000: The Importance of Maintaining a Flow of New Faculty into Academic Research* (Washington, 1979), p. 18. The steady-state distribution is based on assumptions with respect to mortality and retirement that are described in appendix D of this National Research Council report. The steady-state model is useful in illustrating the degree to which faculty in most countries are concentrated in the lower age bracket.

6. Wissenschaftsrat, *Empfehlungen zum Funften Rahmenplan fur den Hochschulausbau,* 1976-1979. *Uberlegungen zur Personnellen Situation de Hochschulen* (Cologne, 1975). This proposal did not outline a program but provided a prognosis and the basic rationale for a program.

7. Deutsche Forschungsgemeinschaft, *Heisenberg Programm zur Forderung des Wissenschaftlichen Nachwuchses: Zweiter Jahresbericht* (internal document; Bonn, 1980).

8. Deutsche Forschungsgemeinschaft, *Merkblatt uber Stipendien des Heisenberg Programm zur Forderung des Wissenschaftlichen Nachwuchses* (Bonn, 17 January 1979; see also the appendix of May 1979).

9. The Higher Education Framework Law, *Hochschulrahmengesetz of 1976,* section 75, subsection 3, provides for the first time some standards binding on the states.

10. Deutsche Forschungsgemeinschaft, *Aufgaben und Finanzierung, 1979-82* (Bonn, 1980), No. 6, p. 167.

11. Science Research Council, *Annual Report, 1978-1979* (London, 1979), p. 4.

13. M. Massenet, *Rapport sur L'Emploi Scientifique, Rapport au Premier Ministre* (Paris: La Documentation Francaise, 1978), p. 83.

14. Projet de Loi de Finances pour 1980, *La Recherche Scientifique et Technique en France en 1980* (Paris: Imprimerie Nationale, 1979), *document annexe,* p. 135.

15. *Le Monde,* January 18, 1980, p. 3.

16. Commissariat General du Plan, *Rapport de la Commission Recherche* (Paris: La Documentation Francaise, 1976), p. 40.

17. Natural Sciences and Engineering Research Council of Canada, *A Five Year Plan for the Programs of the Natural Sciences and Engineering Research Council* (Ottawa, November 1979), Chapter 3, p. 3 and Chapter 4, p. 2.

18. Science Council of Canada, *University Research in Jeopardy, The Threat of Declining Enrollment* (Report 31, Ottawa, 1979).

20. National Research Council, *Nonfaculty Doctoral Research Staff in Science and Engineering* (Washington, 1978).

21. R. Radner and C. Kuh, *Preserving a Lost Generation: Policies to Assure a Steady Flow of Young Scholars Until the Year 2000. A Report and Recommendations* (Berkely, Ca.: Carnegie Council on Policy Studies in Higher Education, October 1978).

22. National Research Council, *Research Excellence through the Year 2000, op. cit.,* p. 37.

23. F. Press, "Universities in the National R&D Efforts," remarks at Florida State University, Tallahassee, April 7, 1978, p. 3 (duplicated).

24. R. Atkinson, "University Research and Graduate Education," remarks to the Annual Meeting of the Eastern Association of Graduate Schools, Albuquerque, N.M., March 7, 1977.

25. R.E. Klitgaard, *The Decline of the Best? An Analysis of the Relationships Between Declining Enrollments, Ph.D. Production and Research,* Discussion Paper 65D, (Cambridge, Mass.: Kennedy School of Government, 1979).

26. Research on which this paper was based was supported by NSF contract PRA 792759.

Engineering,
The Neglected Ingredient

F. Karl Willenbrock

Introduction

Technological progress is vital to the nation's economic health, to the appropriate care of the human environment, and to its national defense. The positive impetus which new technology gives to the economy is recognized both by the business community[1] and by economists. The control and mitigation of hazards to safety and health, the protection of the natural environment, the low-cost availability of natural resources, and many of the amenities of human life are dependent upon improved technologies. In addition, the defense posture of the United States of America is essentially based on the superiority of American weapons technology compared to that of potential adversaries.[2]

Technology is the end-product of the practice of engineering. Thus, the engineering talent available to this country is of crucial importance to its economy, to its quality of living, and to its defense. Both civilian and military technologies draw heavily on engineering talent. In this paper, the character and status of the engineering profession in the United States is explored in order to understand its present strengths and weaknesses, and to examine some of the public policy options available to increase the nation's engineering capability.

Character of Contemporary Engineering

The breadth and diversity of engineering activities are not adequately recognized by the general public. Few members of the public perceive, for example, that the achievements of the National Aeronautical and Space Administration are essentially engineering accomplishments, and that NASA has been accurately described by its former Administrator[3] as an engineering organization that carries out a number of missions, both scientific and technological. Although there have been significant efforts to articulate the nature of engineering,[4] the lack of public comprehension is one of the factors which has led to a

Dr. F. Karl Willenbrock is Cecil H. Green Professor of Engineering and Dean, School of Engineering and Applied Science, Southern Methodist University.

relative neglect of its well-being. Yet, ironically, a recognition of engineering's salient characteristics is necessary for identifying the appropriate methods of strengthening engineering in the United States.

There is no sharp boundary between science and engineering; in fact, under appropriate conditions they are mutually stimulating. For example, the development of the transistor led to a great increase in the understanding of the physics of semiconductors and, in turn, this increase in scientific understanding helped provide the knowledge base necessary for the development of large-scale integrated circuits. However, it is important to recognize that engineering is not simply applied science. Its scope extends far beyond that.

Engineering activities range from research and development to the delivery of goods and services to an end-user. Thus, an engineer must not only operate within the constraints of physical laws, but also within economic constraints. In addition to research and development, which leads to new physical capabilities, engineers must also be adept at cost-effective design and production. They must be able to synthesize new products and services which are successful in the marketplace. Therefore, the engineering enterprise should be viewed both as an academic discipline, involving education and research, and as a professional practice which must meet the technological needs of an end-user. Seventy-eight percent of the engineers in the U.S. are employed in industry. These engineers are primarily involved with design, development, manufacturing, and operational activities which result in products and services which must be competitive in both domestic and international marketplaces.

This century has been characterized by the rapid development of new technologies. While the rate of such developments is one measure of the success of engineering, the practice of engineering has also undergone rapid changes. During the past three decades a notable example has been the development of computing machines. Not only has this development had profound effects on engineering practice, but it has also extended the domain of engineering into new intellectual fields. While the hardware aspects of computing were always recognized as part of engineering, it is now evident that software and systems also essentially fall into the domain of engineering. Thus the domain of engineering expands as new technological products and services are developed. The next major expansion of engineering appears to be in the field of molecular biology, as new organic materials and processes become significant commercially.

Status of Engineering in the United States

While in many technologies the United States is at the forefront of new developments, there are definite indications that U.S. engineering is not in a healthy state. In universities, colleges of engineering suffer from undergraduate enrollments which are too high for available faculty and facilities, graduate enrollments which are too low, and from an inadequate funding base. The lack of appropriate funding is evidenced in the inability of colleges to maintain an adequate number of faculty members, to pay competitive salary levels, and to maintain up-to-date institutional and research facilities.

From the standpoint of the industrial or governmental employer of engineers, there is a severe manpower shortage which will increase as society becomes increasingly dependent upon improved technology. The problem of maintaining the technical skills of practicing engineers at the state of the art is at present only partially solved.

Many individual engineers are not satisfied with either the monetary or the intellectual rewards of a career in engineering. This lack of satisfaction is evidenced in many ways, such as the formation of unions in some companies, the number of engineers who transfer out of engineering, as well as in the pressure exerted on a number of professional societies for engineers to undertake more active roles in improving the financial status and other benefits of its individual members.

In contrast, this country's most active international competitors, in both the industrial and military spheres, are countries in which the engineering profession is carefully nurtured by the national government.

Status of Engineering in Other Industrialized Countries

Comparisons between engineering in the United States and in other industrialized countries can help to illuminate some of the particular strengths and weaknesses of U.S. engineering. The status of engineering in the United Kingdom has recently been subjected to close scrutiny as a result of a two-year study by a Royal Commission chaired by Sir Montague Finniston.[5] A similar study of 18-months' duration was undertaken by the Royal Swedish Academy of Engineering Sciences.[6] Both studies concluded that national industrial capability and international competitiveness depend on the quality and quantity of engineering talent available.

The U.K.'s engineering profession has a number of weaknesses, some of which are also observable in the United States. The engineering profession in Great Britain does not have the social prestige that many other professions have; as a result it is not able to attract the most promising students.[7] Also, industrial engineers are frequently assigned sub-professional tasks, and industries do not press forward aggressively in the use of new technologies. The Finniston Report concluded that it is essential for the United Kingdom to adopt national policies which will strengthen the engineering educational system and also provide improved status to engineers employed in industry.

In contrast, the social prestige associated with an engineering career in France, West Germany, and Japan is high. In France, the competition among the brightest students for entrance to the *Grandes Ecoles* is intense. Medical and engineering careers are the most attractive professions.[8] In West Germany, the social status and salaries associated with academic careers in engineering are high. As a result, technical universities are able to attract very able students into engineering programs and then into graduate studies. Some of the most able of advanced degree recipients are retained as faculty members.

Japan, which has so successfully challenged the United States in producing a number of products featuring advanced technology, graduates a greater actual number of baccalaureate degree engineers than does the United States, although it has one-half the total population. More than 20 percent of the baccalaureate degrees recipients and 40 percent of the master's degree recipients in Japan are engineers; the U.S. percentages are close to five percent in both of these categories. Japan does not devote a major part of its engineering talent to the development of military technology, as the United States does, and so it is not surprising that many Japanese optical, electronic, automotive, and metallurgical products are characterized by superior engineering design and quality at competitive prices.

In the United States, baccalaureate degrees recipients find the gap between industrial salaries and graduate student stipends so great that a decreasing percentage are undertaking graduate work in engineering on a full-time basis. In general, doctoral degree recipients find that industrial positions offer higher salaries and the opportunity to work with more up-to-date facilities. As a result, enrollments of U.S. graduate students in engineering are decreasing, and the best current estimate[9] is that there are two thousand faculty vacancies in engineering colleges.

Specific Problems Facing the Engineering Profession in the United States

Some of the unsolved problems which face the engineering profession in the United States today are:

1. *How to Increase the Attractiveness of Engineering Careers.* While engineering is now attracting an increasing number of highly qualified undergraduate students, it is attracting a decreasing number of the most intellectually capable students to its graduate programs. In order to improve the supply of engineers at all degree levels, it is essential that careers in science and engineering be sufficiently attractive to secondary school students so they will want to take the demanding mathematics and science courses necessary to prepare for these careers.

In many countries, including the USSR, West Germany, and Japan, pre-university students regularly take a much more extensive series of mathematics and science courses than do American students. The importance of improving secondary-school mathematics and science programs and increasing student interest in these fields was emphasized in a recent report to the President by the Secretary of Education and Director of the National Science Foundation.[10]

2. *How to Improve Quality of Undergraduate Engineering Education.* For the past seven years there has been a substantial increase in enrollments in undergraduate engineering and computer programs. While these new students will help reverse the drop in the percentage of engineering baccalaureate degrees granted from ten percent in 1960 to five percent in the late 1970's,[11] engineering colleges are finding it increasingly difficult to provide an educational experience of appropriate quality. A major difficulty is the inability to fill vacant faculty positions;

another is the decrease in full-time graduate enrollments, particularly of American-born students. Thus, the increased teaching load must be borne by a decreased number of graduate teaching assistants whose native tongue is English. Most schools are increasingly dependent on foreign-born teaching assistants, in spite of the fact that many of them lack the language facility needed for good undergraduate teaching.

Another weakness in undergraduate engineering programs is the lack of up-to-date facilities available for laboratory instruction. Engineering education requires a balance between analytical and experimental instruction. As the complexity of experimental equipment has increased, particularly with the advent of computer-controlled instrumentation, a large gap has developed between the experimental facilities used in industrial engineering practice and that available for instruction in engineering schools. If the available laboratory facilities are out-of-date, a natural reaction of the faculty is to deemphasize laboratory-based instruction and to emphasize the more abstract aspect of engineering. While some specialized programs such as cooperative work-study programs can provide undergraduates with experience with up-to-date experimental facilities, only about 15 percent of U.S. engineering undergraduates participate in such programs.

Right now there are major technical areas in which experimental instruction in engineering schools is inadequate. The magnitude of this problem is illustrated by the recent proposal,[12] made by the deans of engineering of the Big Ten universities and one other major engineering college to the Director of the NSF. They called for a special program, with an estimated cost of $100 million, to equip engineering schools in the single area of computer graphics needed for instruction in computer-aided design and computer-aided manufacturing. The lack of adequate instruction in this area is of particular significance when viewed from the standpoint of international competitiveness, since Japan has become the world leader in the use of robotics and other computer-aided manufacturing techniques. These techniques are a major factor in the manufacture of automobiles; in 1980, Japan exceeded the United States for the first time in the number of automobiles manufactured.

Another important area of concern in undergraduate engineering education is the decreasing number of faculty members who have had significant experience in industrial engineering practice. The emphasis on research productivity and on the ability to attract external research funding from federal agencies as criteria for the appointment of engineering faculty members has tended to penalize the prospective faculty member who has devoted a significant period of his career to industrial employment. The effect on undergraduate engineering programs is to make the content of these programs increasingly theoretical in nature, with a corresponding decrease in emphasis on design and practice. The loss of an applications orientation is significant, since most engineering practice is motivated by an effort for improved performance of a product or service at a competitive cost. Another unfortunate result of this change in orientation is to decrease the motivation of applications-oriented students to undertake a concentration in the engineering or computer fields.

3. How to Increase the Quality of Graduate Engineering Education and Research. In contrast to the strong increase in undergraduate enrollments in U.S. engineering schools, there has been a decrease in full-time graduate enrollments at both the master's and doctoral levels. The decreasing percentage of engineering baccalaureate degree recipients who undertake full-time graduate engineering education can be ascribed both to the attractive positions available in industry for baccalaureate degree holders and to the opportunity to undertake graduate work in schools of business and law. Many students are motivated by the conviction that they can, through combining engineering with administrative training, reach higher and more lucrative positions in their industrial careers.

Patterns of graduate education in engineering are strongly influenced by the availability of external sources of funding for research; such funding is available primarily from federal mission agencies and the NSF.[13] Since research in engineering is too expensive to be supported effectively by either university funds or student fees, it is essential for faculty members to obtain additional funding from external sources, if they wish to pursue active research programs and to support their graduate students as research assistants. Currently, over 95 percent of external funding for engineering comes from federal agencies. This funding has strengthened engineering education and university-based research immeasurably, and was a crucial factor in enabling the United States to gain world leadership in many technologies in the post-World War II era. However, most university-based research has been concentrated in those technologies on which the federal agencies' missions depend. For example, the military and space programs are heavily dependent on aerospace, communications, computer, and automatic control technologies. In each of these fields, there are strong university-based research programs, as well as strongly research-and-development-oriented companies which employ the bright students who are attracted to these fields.

In contrast, there are other technological fields in which there is little university-based research and where technological developments have been relatively slow. In such fields, it is difficult to obtain a comprehensive, up-to-date graduate education in the United States. Strong faculty interest has neither developed nor been maintained in these areas, since substantial external funding is not available. Yet some of these fields are of national importance, and their relative neglect has resulted in corresponding weaknesses in the performance of the technology-based U.S. industry.

4. How to Improve the System for Continuing Professional Development for Engineers. A major characteristic of engineering is that the technologies it creates frequently develop at extremely rapid rates. Thus, the problem of keeping engineers up-to-date in their profession, whether they are employed in industry, government, or universities, is a difficult one. Various techniques have been developed by each of these organizations to respond to the problem. Most large industrial organizations have developed extensive internal educational programs. Governmental agencies have developed university interchange programs, and the military services have developed an extensive internal educational system. Universities have developed a system of sabbatical leaves and also allocate a certain percentage of time for faculty members to use for their professional development.

However, each of these organizations has engineers whose usefulness has been substantially reduced due to their not being abreast of current technological developments. Industrial responses to this problem vary from firing members of the engineering staff when they reach the age of 40 and replacing them with more recent engineering graduates, to developing programs which enable middle-aged members of the engineering and administrative staffs to spend extended periods of time in university programs to update their technical skills. Several deans of engineering colleges have estimated that only 30 percent of their faculty members are at present skilled in the use of computers and are effective in teaching computer applications in their courses.

5. *How to Increase Job Satisfaction of Engineers.* While there is little quantitative information available about how engineers feel about their career choice, there are a number of indicators which point to a lack of satisfaction on the part of many engineers. These indicators, mentioned earlier, include the number of unions formed by engineers, the salaries paid engineers during their careers, the number of engineers who leave the profession, and the pressure in some engineering professional societies to direct activities toward bettering the status of individual engineers.

Although reliable data about the number of engineers involved in union activities is not available, there are about 30 companies in the United States with active unions or associations of engineers, according to the current listing of the National Society of Professional Engineers.[14] These organizations use collective-bargaining procedures, and occasionally the unions have resorted to strikes. The salary patterns followed by industrially employed engineers are characterized by substantial increases in the early part of their careers followed by a plateau in a relatively few years.[15] In the academic sector, salary compression is such that well-established, senior professors are paid less than twice the rate paid for newly appointed assistant professors who have just received their Ph.D.

These salary patterns may be one of the explanations for the significant number of engineers who transfer out of engineering positions. In a recent study of engineering manpower issues, based on data of the Bureau of Labor Statistics, Upthegrove[16] projects an annual demand in the next decade for 93,000 engineers. More than half of this demand is created by the choice of presently employed engineers to transfer into nonengineering functions such as management. This out-migration is almost double the annual loss of engineers caused by death and retirement in the 1974-1976 period for which BLS data are available.

Recently, the largest of the engineering professional societies in the United States, the Institute of Electrical and Electronics Engineers, changed its tax status in order to be more active in political activities relating to benefits for its individual members. This further indication of dissatisfaction was undertaken in response to membership demand.

While the extent of the dissatisfaction by members of the engineering profession is not known, the available indicators do not point to a healthy situation in the profession. Rather, it is reasonable to infer that changes are necessary, if the profession is to attract and retain highly capable engineers.

6. How to Improve the Rate of Technological Advance in Some Industrial Sectors. While some industrial sectors are characterized by extremely rapid rates of technological change, other sectors have not experienced much change in technology over many decades. This slow rate of change can be caused by many factors. Slow technological change is usually indicative of relatively little research and development activity within the sector. A low rate of research and development, in turn, frequently results in an inability to attract the most technically capable engineers. In other cases, the market structure, the regulatory environment, the capital investment requirements, or the characteristics of management may have precluded the development and introduction of improved technology.

Some sectors recognize this undesirable situation and act to modify it. For example, the recognition of a lack of systematic research was evident to the electric power industry and resulted in the formation of the Electric Power Research Institute in 1972. Now this institute helps the electric utilities to undertake a more comprehensive research effort than the individual companies or their equipment suppliers were able to previously.

However, other industrial sectors have not developed the strong research and development traditions which have characterized the communications industry, the chemical industry, and the aerospace industry. Areas such as building construction and technologies important to the nation's urban areas have been relatively neglected. In other cases, comprehensive research and development programs have not grown because the industrial structure has not warranted a long-term systematic effort on the part of a single company. In any event, there is a wide range of investment in research and development activities and in the ability of the industrial sectors to advance needed technologies.

7. How to Articulate Needs of the Engineering Profession Effectively. The engineering profession has formed some effective organizational mechanisms which respond to specific needs of the profession. Perhaps most successful are the professional societies. They provide the publications, meetings, and committee structures which keep communications in the various technical fields in a healthy state. These societies have been responsive to new technical developments, so new societies can form easily and existing groups can restructure themselves. The result is that the individual engineer has an effective means of exchanging technical information and can become acquainted with others with the same technical interests.

The professional societies have also helped to develop an effective means of accrediting colleges offering degrees in engineering, and the societies have established some uniformity in requirements for the first degree in engineering. Similarly, trade associations in the industrial sectors provide a means for companies to combine their efforts in the solution of common problems.

However, efforts to form a single organization to represent the interests of all engineers have not yet been successful. Thus, certain critical issues have not been faced, important problems have not been systematically analyzed, and appropriate solutions have not been identified. The latest effort of the professional societies to form an umbrella society resulted in the formation of the American Association of Engineering Societies in January 1980. The organizational structure and funding arrangements engender optimism about this new organization's ability to identify the important issues and to formulate positions in an effective way for presentation in public and private forums.

Public Policy Issues

Engineering is so basic to the development of society's essential technologies that the country cannot allow it to be weakened by chronic unsolved problems, or by public policies inimical to further development. During the post-World War II era, the United States attained leadership both in scientific research and in medical practice. Although the nation's capability is still at the international forefront in some fields, there are other important technological fields in which this country is either lagging behind its leading competitors or is being rapidly overtaken.

The United States can maintain technological leadership only if engineering education, research, and practice are healthy. Problems such as those enumerated in the previous section cannot continue without rendering the profession ineffective in producing essential civilian and military technologies. From the standpoint of public policy, these problems can be grouped into three major categories.

System for Engineering Education

Although much of the higher educational system in the United States suffers from underfunding, this problem is particularly acute in engineering, where the rapid advance of technologies with which engineering education must keep pace has exceeded the financial resources of the universities. Thus engineering colleges are presently unable to:

1. maintain their facilities (laboratory, instruction, and information) at the state of the art;
2. retain on their faculties enough of the most intellectually capable engineers;
3. attract a steady flow of graduate students to supply academic and governmental as well as industrial needs.

Whether sufficient resources can be found to resolve these problems, given the present mode of operation, is uncertain. A major public policy objective should be to strengthen the present educational system through increased financial support and through the development of new ways of sharing costs.

As the chief beneficiary of engineering colleges, technology-based industrial companies are prime candidates for increasing support to engineering colleges. While the industrial sector currently assists universities in a variety of ways, the scope and magnitude of their assistance could be increased. Such assistance must be of direct benefit to the companies involved, since they operate on a for-profit basis.

A number of possibilities merit consideration and investigation. If students were able to gain some of their experience in an industrial environment, rather than attempting to keep college laboratory equipment up-to-date in all instructional areas, a tremendous burden could be lifted from engineering colleges. Such action would resemble teaching hospitals where medical students receive part of their education in the environment where medicine is practiced and where the facilities are kept at the state of the art. An experiment involving "teaching companies" has been underway in the United Kingdom for a number of years, with the support of the Science Research Council. While such a possibility may not be applicable to all engineering colleges in the United States, it could work in specific technical fields. The government role here would be as facilitator and as a source of initial funding.

The possibility of joint university-industry use of facilities for research is also worthy of investigation. A recent National Science Foundation study[17] documented the current gap between industrial laboratory facilities and, even, the leading university laboratories. In its recent report on cooperative research relations between industry and universities, the National Commission on Research[18] lists a number of recommendations for further investigation.

In addition, the attractiveness of engineering faculty positions could be increased with the assistance of the industrial sector. Current research funding practices of federal agencies result in faculty members devoting much time and effort to seeking external funding. In effect, most faculty members must reestablish annually the value of their research programs, while also coping with the handicaps of outdated facilities and inadequate technician support. Joint university-industry research programs could be refashioned to ameliorate this problem. The NSF's University-Industry Cooperation Program is an example of a small, current program which furthers this objective. Moreover, the possible use of DOD's Independent Research and Development (IR&D) program to support university-based research could have a major effect in strengthening university programs.

Finally, there is clearly a need for improving both the quality and quantity of graduates of the engineering educational system. The whole gamut of programs which prepare students for engineering careers must be made sufficiently attractive so that increasing numbers of the brightest students participate. However, this education is only the starting point of a career in engineering, and the industrial companies determine the environment and the rewards for the major part of the profession. Unless prospective students see the possibility of having productive and satisfying careers, they will not be attracted to graduate programs in engineering, and, as a consequence, neither engineering colleges, nor industrial and governmental employers, will have access to the nation's top intellectual talent. To improve this situation, efforts of the industrial and university sectors must cooperate, with governmental encouragement and support.

Static Technological Fields

An examination of the significant technologies in today's economy indicates that the United States is at the forefront of a number of them, including aerospace, computers, telecommunications, chemical processing, and agriculture. However, there is an increasing number of fields in which the United States is not a leader or where it has been recently displaced from a front-rank position. Some examples of these fields include optics, steel, consumer electronics, and automobiles. While it is not reasonable to assume that U.S. technology will lead the world in all fields, it is important that the United States be near the leading position in technical areas of fundamental importance to the U.S. industrial economy and its national defense.

Many of the fields in which the U.S. engineering position is strong are those in which the technologies involved are basic to the mission of major federal agencies, which therefore support university-based research and make use of the technology developed. Programs connected with these fields have resulted in a continuing flow of new knowledge and a supply of highly capable graduates. Since these agencies, such as the Department of Defense and NASA, are also major customers for the products of these technologies, the new knowledge is used directly and capable students are able to contribute directly as full-time engineers upon graduation.

There are also fields of current U.S. engineering strength in which federal agencies are not the major consumers of the technological output. In agriculture, where the U.S. position is particularly dominant, a university-based research program combines with an effective system of diffusing new knowledge to the farming community. In telecommunications, the market structure is such that an effective research and development effort has been maintained, primarily in the private sector, for many decades. Similarly, in the chemical processing and petroleum industries, there has been little public funding involved, but these industries have continued their development and are technologically advanced.

In contrast, there are other industries in which there is little systematic technological development. These are frequently characterized by relatively slow changes in technology and low productivity. While some have little impact on the general health of the U.S. economy, there are also fields of direct importance where there has not been enough public or private sector support. Examples of these fields are manufacturing technology (including robotics and building construction), urban technology (including water supply and waste disposal systems), and the quality control of products and services. Here the national investment should be increased to a level commensurate with overall public interest. Public policy makers should see which new institutional mechanisms, like the generic technology centers provided for in the Stevenson-Wydler Technological Innovation Act of 1980 (PL 96-480), or, more indirectly, like tax incentives or the encouragement of industrial consortia, are likely to be most effective.

While support of fundamental research at universities has been firmly established in both federal legislation and federal agency policy, public policies need to be clarified when the research results are closer to commercial applications. This area has been studied both by the Research and Policy Committee of the Committee for Economic Development and by the National Commission on Research, but as yet no clear policy has been articulated.

The understandable effort on the part of the Congress and the Office of Management and Budget to avoid displacing private funding of research with public monies has resulted in a number of technological gaps. Closing these gaps will require judicious development of federal policies in which the roles for government, industry, academia, and not-for-profit research institutes are clearly defined. Effective working relationships must be developed. The nation cannot afford to neglect important technological fields simply because they do not coincide with the missions of research-funding federal agencies or because the private sector does not support them adequately.

Inadequate Availability of Engineering Manpower

Generally, problems of manpower are usually considered solely a question of too few engineering graduates; however, it is increasingly clear that the updating and retention of presently practicing engineers is also a major concern. Right now, the outflow of engineers from the profession is almost equal to the input of new graduates. Thus, there is no systematic build-up of engineering capability in the United States, which characterizes some of the nation's most successful competitors in technology.

Developing an adequate flow of engineering graduates at all degree levels will require the combined efforts of the academic, industrial, and governmental sectors: engineering colleges must provide efficient and effective educational programs at both the undergraduate and graduate levels; industrial employers must eliminate boom-and-bust hiring practices; and governmental support should enable engineering colleges and industrial companies to carry out these objectives.

The rapid rate of technological change presents a difficult career problem for all practicing and academic engineers. Although new information-handling technology, such as closed-circuit television and videotape, has helped in teaching, such developments are only partially effective, and are not sufficiently built into the career patterns of practicing professionals. Scientific and technical obsolescence remains a significant problem throughout the engineering profession. The cooperation of universities, professional societies, and employers of engineers will be needed to bring about a comprehensive attack on the problem of technical obsolescence. Since the federal government is both a direct employer and an indirect employer of engineering talent through its contracts with technology-based industry, it has a substantial interest in improving the present situation.

The intellectual skills of engineers must be maintained at a high level so that employers, whether industrial, academic, or governmental, will use engineers in increasingly effective ways. At the same time, engineers will find their work intellectually stimulating, and their rates of compensation should increase throughout their careers. Until this mutually beneficial point is reached, the engineering profession will not be able to attract and retain the quality of professional personnel necessary to maintain the U.S. in its technological leadership.

REFERENCES

1. See, for example, *Stimulating Technological Progress,* a statement by the Research and Policy Committee of the Committee for Economic Development, January 1980.

2. "William Perry and the Weapons Gamble," *Science,* February 13, 1980, p. 81.

3. Robert A. Frosch, Annual Meeting of the National Academy of Engineering, October 1980.

4. S.C. Florman, *The Existential Pleasures of Engineering,* (New York: St. Martin's Press, 1976.)

5. "Engineering: Our Future," Report of the Committee of Inquiry into the Engineering Profession, Sir Montague Finniston, Chairman, January 1980.

6. "Technical Capability and Industrial Competence," Report by the Royal Swedish Academy of Engineering Sciences (IVA), Gunnar Hambraeus, President, June 1979.

7. "The Engineering Profession, a National Investment," Report of Working Party of the Conservative Party chaired by Professor John Thornton, July 1978.

8. Private communication from Professor Jean L.M. Michel, *Ecole Nationale des Ponts et Chaussees,* France.

9. Private communication from Dr. Henry Bourne, Deputy Assistant Director of Engineering and Applied Science, NSF.

10. *Science and Engineering Education for the 1980's and Beyond,* Report to the President by the National Science Foundation and the Department of Education, October 1980.

11. "Science and Engineering Personnel: a National Overview," NSF Report 80-316.

12. Letter from Dean Donald D. Glower to Dr. R.C. Atkinson, Director, National Science Foundation, August 9, 1978, including a Position Statement by Big Ten and Stanford University Deans of Engineering.

13. See, for example, F. Karl Willenbrock, "The Impact of Federal Research Funding on Schools of Engineering in the United States," in *National Science & Technology Policy Issues,* April 1979, Report of the House Committee on Science and Technology, 96th Congress.

14. Private communication from Milton F. Lunch, General Counsel, National Society of Professional Engineers, and NSPE Tabulation of Unions Representing Engineering and Technical Employees, Revised January 1980.

15. Engineering Manpower Commission, "Professional Income of Engineers, 1980," American Association of Engineering Societies, New York, November 1980.

16. William R. Upthegrove, "Engineering Manpower Issues: Must It Always be Feast or Famine," *Business-Higher Education Forum,* 1 DuPont Circle, Washington, D.C., March 1980.

17. L. Berkowitz *et al.,* "Instrumentation Needs of Research Universities," *Science,* March 6, 1981, p. 1013.
18. "Industry and the Universities: Developing Cooperative Research Relationships in the National Interest," Report of the National Commission on Research, August 1980.

Quantitative Methods in Research and Development Decision-Making

Carolyn Heising-Goodman

Introduction

In the United States today, the debate over how to solve the energy problem has many aspects; one of the key aspects is the sub-debate over how decisions regarding research and development should be made. One side of the argument, presented independently by Lovins,[1] Taylor,[2] and Kneese,[3] is that such decisions should be made essentially devoid of and apart from what many would call the scientific method of decision-making and remain entirely embedded in the existing political process. These critics of the scientific method argue that analysis, particularly in its cost-benefit application, fails to integrate important aspects of policy questions and therefore leads to erroneous conclusions.[4] They hold that quantitative, scientific approaches to public policy analysis are too narrow in scope and prohibit the projection of intuitive knowledge into the formulation of models. In addition, they argue that quantitative methods cannot handle issues that are ethical in nature, and, in fact, may obscure such issues.

The ethical question in the energy debate (and in the sub-debate over methods for decision-making) has been eloquently addressed by the complementary thinkers Margaret N. Maxey and David J. Rose. These authors contend that ethics and science are *not* separate entities, and that scientific approaches to resolution of issues and of decision-making in the energy field and elsewhere are, in fact, quite ethical. Dr. Maxey succintly observes:[5, 6]

> What is really at issue in risk assessment methodologies is not the propriety or impropriety of putting some callous "dollar value" on human life or injury as a moral judgment of individual worth, much less of economic losses to society as a measure of personal expendability. The public should have long since been confronted with a *threefold ethical justification for cost/risk/benefit quantifications* [emphasis added], namely:
> 1. we are in fact maximizing the value we as a society place on human life when we endeavor to allocate public monies in such a way as to reduce widespread hazards, thereby preventing as much loss of life and protection from injury as possible;

Dr. Carolyn Heising-Goodman is a Research Associate of the Nuclear Engineering Department at the Massachusetts Institute of Technology.

2. by utilizing this method, we minimize arbitrary, piecemeal, isolated, selective decisions, and instead aim at the most socially responsive and responsible process of decision-making about the cost-effectiveness of finite resources and public revenues;

3. with this method we have visible and verifiable standards for judging the accountability of elected or appointed officials in their allocation of public monies in a just and equitable manner.

Professor Rose echoes similar themes from a different standpoint in his Killian lectures delivered at MIT and elsewhere:[7, 8] "Faith and grace are necessary but only the other side of reason and responsibility; the duty falls on us and we are damned to shirk it, waiting for God or chance to rescue us." He warns of "selective attention" in not seeing the larger problem because too much attention is placed on one or another part instead of the whole, and he warns against the myopic time perspectives and the "looking good syndrome" of those involved in the political process:

> The pressure of election leads to time perspectives of only a few years, for example five, a myopia that is occasionally moderated by some politician's sense of history. ... Responsive to some complex socio-technological issue, on which perhaps much conflicting information appears to exist, someone in a position of influence or authority calls for a study to be made to address the questions, either afresh, anew, or again. So our heroes in academia, industria, national laboratoria, or foundatia go to work, carefully listing the facts and perceptions pro and con in their report. What happens? *The sponsor before the start had a prior opinion, and never any intention to change it* [emphasis added]. All he does is run quickly through the report, selecting passages and views that support the preconception; the rest goes in the waste basket. ... So grows the amount of information, the degree of polarization, and the irresolution of many issues. All becomes painted black or white; the call goes out for more studies, upon which the antagonists feed afresh by selective inattention. From here it is but a short mental step to the "looking good" syndrome, where the principal aim is cosmetic. Whether something useful gets done can become incidental.

These observations by Maxey and Rose point out at once both the promise and the challenge of integrating quantitative data, scientific methods and expertise into the political process, where many of the country's major R&D decisions are made. The alternative to attempting such integration is to continue with "business as usual," a less desirable choice. For, contrary to what their critics assert, quantitative approaches to analyzing important policy questions are among the best available, and decision processes which incorporate these approaches are far better than those that choose to ignore such methods.

Traditional Methods Used in R&D Decision-Making

Long-range research and development are exceptionally uncertain. The utility of a potential product often depends upon a host of circumstances about which there exists great doubt. Uncertainties around both demand and supply for a product can change drastically, as can early estimates of performance and project costs. As an R&D program proceeds, original designs and plans invariably change; unforeseen technical difficulties forestall the meeting of performance requirements. Yet despite all the uncertainties, decisions must be made. The way the decision makers deal with uncertainty may well determine the overall success of the program.

Considerable uncertainties also occur on the supply side. Early estimates of performance, cost of development and production, and of availability are usually inaccurate and biased. Costly product modifications are required to keep pace with an ever-changing environment. Hence, early predictions based on initial design inevitably require revision. In most government studies of project fund allocation and optimal program timing, deterministic models are often developed that give estimate ranges on a "High," "Medium" and "Low" scale — the judgment of which value is most likely to occur is left up to the reader. Yet, expertise *can* be brought to bear on even the problem of ranking the relative importance of estimates; since such judgments can be made intuitively, the question becomes one of encoding the best available estimates of those who are most knowledgeable on the subject — the experts.

The traditional method for dealing with R&D planning has given government a central role in setting priorities; the Executive branch and the President generally set the tone and direction in which the country will move. Congress is left with perhaps the more rudimentary and less awe-inspiring (but equally important) task of approving budgets and appropriating funds. It is not infrequently that the priorities of the presidential administration tend to clash with the more multi-valued perspective that Congress represents; these battles can rage for a good many years with both sides hoping to gain the edge in power required to upset the other.

In the area of energy, R&D goals have often been determined by influential individuals (or pressure groups) capable of selling a promising idea or philosophy,* sometimes with little intent of pushing an idea that has any true merit in the real world. Professor Rose notes a curiously appropriate example of such mischievous antics in his Killian lectures:

> ... A prominent U.S.S.R. scientist working on controlled fusion promoted his view strongly that the route to success lay in developing particular pulsed devices that combined both fusion and breeding of fissionable material. The concept was infeasible; being clever and realistic, he certainly knew it. Why then did he do it? He saw it as strongly attractive to many in the political and administrative sectors who could not understand the infeasibility; using the idea, he could therefore advance himself *and be well out of the way before things fell apart* [emphasis added]. Perhaps he could even blame the poor wretch who had been left in charge and had clearly ruined the concept. That particular scientist is now a vice-chairman of the Soviet Academy of Sciences.[7]

---

*See, for example, R.J. Rydell's interesting review of the politics behind the decisions to move toward the breeder in the United States and Britain.[9] Perhaps a more apropos example might be the push toward solar and "small is beautiful" technology in the U.S. as reflected by the Carter Administration's budget requests for energy R&D.[10]

Perhaps there is a lesson here for those who would rely on too narrow a base of expert opinion — or who take too seriously the words of the latest public demagogue.

To avoid such problems, a broader base of expertise must be called upon; credibility is enhanced by hard data and facts from a multitude of sources, and must be relied upon over the seductive tones and wishful thinking of many political advocates. How to decide who is "telling the truth"? Look for those with the long-term societal responsibility for their actions — not only are they more likely to be conservative and truthful in their advocacy, but they are apt to be around later to take responsibility for their earlier actions.

The R&D process consists of five basic problem-solving activities: 1. definition of the problem; 2. devising solutions; 3. implementing the solutions; 4. evaluating the success of the solutions; and 5. assessing the effect of the solution on other problem areas. On the one hand, R&D can be seen as a system of inquiry geared toward attaining a higher level of understanding prior to a definitive solution of a particular problem. On the other hand, it can be viewed as a political process, where conflicting interests and attitudes interact to yield outcomes which may be satisfactory or acceptable to all concerned parties but without necessarily any increase in the understanding of the fundamental problems.

There is a distinction to be made here between the questions of scientific fact versus questions of scientific direction. Whereas the researcher concerns him or herself with the more finite and substantive questions of research, the managers of science concern themselves with the larger, less tangible questions of scientific direction. Where should the analytic machine of science be directed, and what problems should it address? Managers of science, often former "hard" scientists (or engineers) themselves, gain acceptance of their ideas on these questions via political suasion; hence, the political side of R&D. For example, Edison was more than an inventor and brilliant applied scientist — he was also a manager and director of scientific advancement. The days when one person can be both may well be over; although one can start a company to commercialize an idea, the larger the company grows, the greater becomes the gulf between the pure scientist and the administrator of science. When the government became involved in science and the process of technological development during World War II, it became more difficult to distinguish science from politics as methods for problem solving. Some might agree, then, that the R&D process is best seen as a "unique form of politics."[9]

The history of operations research and the quantitative approach to policy-making, including decisions involving R&D, also began in the war years of the 1940's. Evolving out of defense planning for distribution and production of wartime equipment and goods, operations research first dealt deterministically and linearly with problems of resource allocation. George Dantzig, father of linear programming, in his memoirs of these early times once remarked that his was a linearized world of objective functions subject to constraints of an unique nature. Since those productive days of von Neumann, Dantzig and others, the field has both broadened and grown, becoming both probabilistic and non-linear.

Operations research is applied to problems that concern operations or activities conducted within an organization.[11] The approach of operations research is scientific. The process begins by carefully observing and formulating the problem and then constructing a scientific (typically mathematical) model that attempts to abstract the essence of the problem. It is then hypothesized that this model is a sufficiently precise representation of the essential features of the situation, so conclusions (solutions) obtained from the model are also valid for the real problem. This hypothesis is then modified and verified by suitable experimentation. Thus, in a certain sense, operations research also is concerned with the practical management of the organization. Operations research attempts to find the best or optimal solution to the problem under consideration. Rather than being content with merely improving the "status quo," the goal is to identify the best possible course of action. Although it must be interpreted carefully, the "search for optimality" is a very important theme in operations research.

Methods Available for Policy Analysis: a Bayesian Approach

Among the many methods for operations research available in deciding between projects, allocating funds, and determining time schedules, the probabilistic approach of Bayesian decision analysis emerges as very promising. The Bayesian perspective asserts that uncertainty reflects a subjective state-of-mind or state-of-knowledge; this perspective lends itself naturally to an interesting viewpoint on the value of research and development. Although all management functions must cope with uncertainty, R&D is generally agreed to be the function involving both the largest number and widest range of uncertainties. Thus, the R&D manager faces huge problems, not only in selecting the most promising avenues for R&D effort and expenditure, but also in attempting to ensure a steady flow of technically successful projects. The lengthening time scale of R&D work exacerbates the uncertainty and complexity of this management effort. Frequently, five to ten years or more may be required to achieve technical success, and an additional five to ten years to realize full commercial potential. Nevertheless, despite substantial uncertainties, it is possible to estimate future success effectively. For, if uncertainty is to be reduced, state-of-knowledge must be improved, and this is only possible through experimentation and through the consultation of experts.

From this perspective, an R&D decision based on the best available state-of-knowledge is accomplished through the consultation of experts whose consensus opinion provides a basis upon which to act. Balthasar, et al.[12] suggest that "subjective probability judgments are a reliable guide to future events and thus management should use them as the basis for R&D planning and decisions." A major benefit of an explicitly quantitative approach is that it synthesizes the opinions of a diverse group of experienced experts more effectively than alternative qualitative approaches. Another advantage is that many models and techniques to aid management in planning and controlling R&D projects require probabilities of success as one of their major inputs. A further advantage is that one can make a probability distribution on the output of the entire R&D process and depict the expected success of the R&D function in terms of the number of new developments expected to be ready for commercialization in each of the following years, thereby providing a current indicator of intermediate and long-term results. Similar distributions can be developed for R&D expenditures, future applicability and effectiveness of the R&D results, as well as for other parameters of interest both to R&D and to upper management.

Explicit numerical representations of expert opinion are a regular input concerning the evaluation of important R&D problems in the approach based on subjective probability. A substantial literature exists recommending subjective probability judgment as the most appropriate basis for decision-making under uncertainty (see, for example, the work of the Stanford Research Institute's Decision Analysis group).[13] Much of the theoretical basis for this approach comes from the influential work of Reverend Thomas Bayes, a brilliant statistician and thinker who lived in England in the 1750s. Reverend Bayes devised a theorem by which the state-of-information existing prior to the decision or problem at hand could be updated with new information gained either through direct experimentation or upon consultation with experts. The result of the new information combined with the old is called the *posterior* information, and in mathematics is usually a probability distribution of some type.* His theorem, and its later interpretation by others, provides the foundation upon which the Bayesian approach to probability and statistics is based. That is, Bayesians view probability as a reflection of the state-of-knowledge of a given phenomenon — if perfect information were known, then all "uncertainty" would vanish. Bayesians assert that statements on likelihood, frequencies and probabilities simply reflect an imperfect state-of-knowledge, and that therefore probability is a "state-of-mind" and not a "state-of-matter." From this perspective, then, the approach of encoding an expert's estimates of subjective probability on various important but uncertain parameters is theoretically justifiable. Moreover, in common practice, the Bayesian approach can be shown to be quite representative of what is usually done anyway in coming to decisions.

The process of encoding probability is one that usually involves intensive interviews of experts by analysts. The SRI Decision Analysis group has established methods for accomplishing the transformation of expert opinion into the quantitative probability distributions required to apply decision analysis methods. Spetzler and Stael von Holstein[15] have described the probability encoding methods currently used by SRI, which are based on several years of experience, as well as

---

*For a detailed description of the Bayesian approach to statistics contrasted to two other prevalent approaches, see Efron's paper on controversies in the foundations of statistics.[14]

on evidence from experiments. One such method is based on the use of a probability "wheel," which is a disk with two sectors, one blue and the other red, with a fixed pointer in the center of the disk. The disk is spun, finally stopping with the pointer either in the blue or the red sector. A simple adjustment changes the relative size of the two sectors and thereby also the probabilities of the pointer which indicates either sector when the disk stops spinning. The subject is asked whether he would prefer to bet either on an event relating to the uncertain quantity, e.g., that next year's production will not exceed x units, or on the pointer ending up in the red sector. The amount of red in the wheel is then varied until the expert becomes indifferent. When indifference is established, the relative amount of red is assigned as the probability of the event. This use of the probability wheel is called a "reference process," whereby the subject can relate his probability judgment to a tangible reference point that more easily visualizes the encoding process.

In utilizing the Bayesian approach, it is important that the expertise used in the analysis be carefully scrutinized for validity and appropriateness; a high-energy physicist is not a nuclear scientist, just as a psychologist is not a sociologist; though the areas are related, the best available expert in one area must be relied upon over others in related but separate areas. Expertise must be incorporated in such a way as to minimize any overt biases an individual expert may harbor.

R&D forecasters seem to fall into two categories:[12] those who feel capable of giving direct numerical assignments to future possibilities and those who have difficulty in making such judgments. Most people tend to fall initally into the second category. For this reason, indirect response techniques like the probability wheel are generally a better way to begin encoding. Later, when the forecaster is more familiar with the process, he or she often prefers to assign probabilities directly to the events.*

Judgmental probabilities, though subjective, can be represented in an objective form, that is, as numbers on a scale form 0 to 1 (or 0% to 100%). For example, suppose that there are three current R&D projects, each having an assigned subjective probability of success of 0.4. Assume also that in the future, 0, 1, 2, or 3 of these projects will in fact succeed, with probabilities 0.126, 0.432, 0.288, and 0.064, respectively. This is a probability distribution with an expected value of (0.216 x 0 + 0.432 x 1 + 0.288 x 2 + 0.064 x 3) = 1.2; i.e. 1.2 out of the three projects are expected to succeed. In general, as in the example, the expected number of successful projects is precisely the sum of success probabilities of the individual projects. Note that while the expected value is seldom an integer, and therefore is seldom achievable, it does measure the average result that would be achieved by a large number of similar research efforts.[12]

---

*For rare event estimation, none of the available standard probability encoding techniques work well. In this case, probabilistic modelling is more effective than simple encoding; an example of such "modelling" is that of WASH-1400, *The Reactor Safety Study.*[16]

Application of the Method to Energy Planning: R&D Decisions in Nuclear Energy

Technology assessments of risks and benefits of an energy technology can be of great use in determing the relative importance of R&D funding for competing technologies, both within and outside a general category of technology (e.g., coal versus solar; within nuclear, light water reactors versus liquid metal fast breeder reactors). Traditionally, in the public sector such decisions are made by the President and Congressional committees; assessments are not likely to change this decision-making process, but can aid such a process. For example, if risk studies indicate that solar technologies are "riskier" (in one sense or another) than say, nuclear technologies, such studies might be used to justify modifications in R&D budgets. (This example is given because conventional wisdom may, in fact, be faulty.) Studies that go against conventional ideology and broad public sentiment will be, of course, controversial. But decisions should at least be based in part on the best technical studies available. The alternative is to always defer to majority rule, no matter how misguided. Such questions are for the political scientists to ponder; the technologist can only continue to perform the studies and hope that somebody listens.

R&D managers, both in and out of the public sector, are caught in the curious position of being the middle men between the pure technologists and the political actors at "the top." Whether they choose to ignore or to accept a study result depends on two factors: 1. how well the study was done from a technical perspective (how it handles expert opinion, etc.), and 2. how well the study was received by upper management. Controversy surrounding the Reactor Safety Study (WASH-1400) demonstrates these points (implicitly, WASH-1400 was based on a Bayesian statistical perspective). For example, the Lewis committee, the peer-review group convened by the Nuclear Regulatory Commission to make recommendations on the methods and results of WASH-1400, simultaneously advocated the extension of fault/event tree methods in the nuclear regulatory process, and suggested that WASH-1400 erred significantly in understating the error bounds on reactor accident frequencies.[17] In response to these comments, Professor Rasmussen, in his testimony before the House committee on Interior and Insular Affairs,[18] pointed out that although the uncertainties in WASH-1400 are somewhat "understated," the degree of understatement can only be slightly greater (and not "significantly" greater) than the upper limit of the WASH-1400 estimate. He supports his observations by looking at data of existing experience and a study by Apostolakis and Mosleh[19] on core melt frequency, which incorporates 310 reactor-years of experience, the Browns Ferry fire, expert opinion in WASH-1400, and WASH-1400 itself.

One substantial effort to encode values on a number of important "key uncertainties" and to test decision sensitivity to such values was undertaken by Richels and Manne.[20] It calculated the economic benefits of nuclear fuel reprocessing and the breeder reactor. The author went one step further to show how risk could be balanced against benefits, including such "intangibles" as proliferation risk.[21] These studies demonstrate how quantitative methods can be applied to difficult questions in the R&D decision-making process, particularly in the energy area. In Richels and Manne's work, for example, decision analysis was used to evaluate four alternative R&D strategies: *1.* concurrent development of the Clinch River Breeder Reactor (CRBR) demonstration plant and commercial prototype (PLBR); *2.* sequential development of the CRBR and PLBR; *3.* delay until better information becomes available; and *4.* stopping the R&D program altogether. Only option *1* leads to the first commercial breeder reactor (CBR-1) by 1995. With the sequential development and "delay" options, CBR-1 is not available until 2000 and 2005, respectively. Richels and Manne used a set of judgmental probabilites on a number of important key uncertainties (electricity demand, uranium availability, capital costs of breeder versus light-water reactor, etc.) to determine the optimal alternative. They also conducted a stochastic sensitivity analysis to indicate decision sensitivity to each key parameter. On the basis of their best estimates, they found alternative *1,* concurrent development, to be optimal.

The author made an attempt[21] to extend Richels and Manne's efforts by including the relationship between the decision concerning the reprocessing of spent fuel and the breeder decision in the economic calculation of benefits; half the time for this analysis was spent in quantifying the risks involved with plutonium reactor systems. These risks include health, safety, safeguards, and proliferation categories, with the greatest emphasis placed on the categories or safeguard and proliferation. The author also used Bayesian decision analysis, defining three alternative decisions available to the U.S. (through the President and Congress) with regard to reprocessing and the breeder: to permit, to delay, and to prohibit. Benefits and costs for each alternative were evaluated and compared in dollar terms to determine the optimal decision. Mathematical models helped assess both reprocessing and breeder economic benefits to the U.S. Results show that the social costs due to all categories of risk, with the exception of proliferation, are less than the economic benefits by more than one thousand times, and that permit dominates both options of delay and prohibit. Including proliferation under the conservative assumptions used in the analysis resulted in a factor of approximately seven between cost and benefits. Thus, on the basis of the analysis, it appeared that the permit option is optimal. (The United States is actually following the prolonged delay alternative, while France, the U.S.S.R., Japan, the U.K., and West Germany move ahead with the permit alternative.) These studies demonstrate how Bayesian decision analysis can be constructively applied to analyze even the most difficult of R&D decisions (indicating also how difficult the effectual incorporation of such study results can be in the existing political process).

How Quantitative Methods Can Be Integrated
Into Federal Research Policy Decision-Making Process

The use of risk-analysis methods is becoming widely accepted in the area of regulation, particularly in nuclear power applications. Economic methods are used extensively to provide estimates of the potential benefits for specific projects. Combined, these approaches can assess priorities among any set of competing projects. Expert opinion and public value judgments can also be quantitatively included in these analyses to help reflect the best available knowledge and the past and present attitudes of society. Risk acceptability levels and perceptions of benefit may also fluctuate with time; these uncertainties can also be handled quantitatively. The results of these analyses can help guide the decision-making process. They do not replace this process. Problems of a political type, such as pressures from suasion by peers and others, will still exist; there is no substitute for our present political system. However, greater application of quantitative approaches can lead to greater acceptance and credibility for the help these processes give in minimizing undesirable influences. Properly integrated and exercised, techniques for technology assessment can be very powerful and useful in the most complicated of situations.

REFERENCES

1. Amory Lovins, "Cost-Risk-Benefit Assessments in Energy Policy," *George Washington Law Review,* Vol. 45, No. 5, August 1977, pp. 917-943.

2. Vince Taylor, "Subjectivity and Science: A Correspondence About Belief," *Technology Review,* February 1979, pp. 49-57.

3. A.V. Kneese, "The Faustian Bargain," *Resources,* No. 44, September 1973, pp. 1-8.

4. For another view, see Carolyn D. Heising-Goodman, "Analysis vs. Subjectivity," *Technology Review,* December/January 1980, pp. 2-4. This letter is a response to the article by Vincent Taylor cited above.

5. M.N. Maxey, "Energy Needs: A Bioethical Perspective on Value-Conflicts," Address Given at American Nuclear Society Topical Meeting on Thermal Nuclear Reactor Safety, Knoxville, Tennessee, April 1980.

6. M.N. Maxey, "Radiation Protection Philosophy: Bioethical Problems and Priorities," *American Industrial Hygiene Association Journal,* Vol. 39, September 1980, pp. 689-694.

7. David J. Rose, "Energy — Some Unasked Questions — Continuity and Metanoia," The James R. Killian, Jr. Faculty Achievement Lectures, Massachusetts Institute of Technology, April 1980.

8. David J. Rose, "On the Global CO2 Problem," Testimony to U.S. Senate, Committee on Energy and Natural Resources, April 3, 1980.

9. Randy J. Rydell, "Decision-Making on the Breeder Reactor in Britain and the United States," unpublished Ph.D. Thesis, Princeton University, October 1979.

10. U.S. Congress, House of Representatives, Committee on Science and Technology, "1980 Department of Energy Authorizations," Hearings, 96th Congress, First Session, February — March 1979, Vols. II-IV.

11. F.S. Hillier and G.J. Lieberman, *Operations Research,* 2nd Ed., (San Fran-